WELCOME TO THE FIRST DAY OF YOUR NEW LIFE

THIS PLANNER BELONGS TO:

Name:_____

HOW TO USE THIS PLANNER

so you can totally rock it!

This planner isn't really just a planner... which you'll come to see.
This "planner" is going to start with a series of activities and
worksheets to really help you understand yourself and what it is
you want out of this one miraculous life!
Plus if you don't know that then what the hell are you really
planning for?
I know this planner will help you feel more organized, help you
create better habits, and learn to love the one you are! But my
true hope is that you finish this planner with a sense of purpose
and a knowing that you have the strength to go for your dreams
so you never look back on your life with regret!
Enjoy Your New Planner (& Life) xoxo

Julia

*P.s. Remember you're striving for **progress, not perfection!***

THE SELF HELP PLANNER

This Planner is unlike anything you've ever used!
So before you get started I want to give you a little overview of how this
Planner is set up. The Planner is broken up into 4 sections

LIFE IS

BETTER

WITH A PLAN

Section 1.1
The Life Proof Plan

WHAT IS A
LIFE PROOF PLAN?

Do you know that feeling when you're about to fall asleep and start to think about everything you want to do the next day? Then the next day, you wake up and get sucked into your day without getting anything you wanted done?

I know we all blame not having the "motivation" but the truth is we don't have a plan or a plan that will work. Until the *Life Proof Plan* that is!

The Life-Proof Plan is made up of 3 parts.

Plan A, Plan B, and the Oh Shit Plan.

Unlike most plans, the Life-Proof Plan is designed for failure! You won't only have something to keep you on track but you'll have had a plan for when you fall off track. And trust me at some point you will fall off track, and that's totally allowed because you know, you're a human after all!

On the next page, I give you an example of how the Life-Proof Plan is set up! Use this as a reference when creating your Life-Proof Plan but be sure to tailor the plan to fit your life and your needs!

P.s. The Life-Proof Plan can be used for ANYTHING but I want you to create this plan specifically around using this planner!

LIFE PROOF PLAN?

WHERE I WILL COMPLETE &
WHAT I NEED TO COMPLETE

I Will Complete my planner and Activities on my kitchen island I
will need my book, pens, and a cute basket to keep it all in

MY PLAN A

My Plan A is to
complete my Planner
& Activities in the
morning while I drink
my coffee!

Bonus
Try to work your plan into
something you already do
every day! i.e. drinking coffee

MY PLAN B

If I skip a Moring
that's totally fine
because My Plan B is..
to complete my
Planner & Activities at
night before I go to
bed!

OH SHIT PLAN

If I skip a Moring and at
night that's totally fine
because My Oh Shit
Plan is to...
Double Down the Next
Day day in the morning
while I drink my coffee!

LIFE PROOF PLAN?

WHERE I WILL COMPLETE &
WHAT I NEED TO COMPLETE

_____
_____
_____

MY PLAN A	MY PLAN B	OH SHIT PLAN

JUST A FEW FRIENDLY REMINDERS...
BECAUSE SOMETIMES WE ALL FORGET

GROWTH IS
UNCOMFORTABLE
BECAUSE YOU'VE NEVER
BEEN HERE BEFORE-
YOU'VE NEVER BEEN THIS
VERSION OF YOU. SO GIVE
YOURSELF A LITTLE
GRACE AND BREATHE
THROUGH IT.

-KRISTIN LOHR

TRACK YOUR PROGRESS

Section 1.2
The Life Wheel

WHAT IS A LIFE WHEEL?

You know that one person who lost a bunch of weight or who started a business and it took off? Each person had all had different ways to track their small successes, which helped keep them going! whether it was losing 5lbs or getting that first sale, they had ways to track their success. With self-growth, it's hard to track your progress or even to know where you stand in the first place.

That's why I love the life wheel! It gives you a visual of where you are so you can understand what areas you really want to improve. Plus over time you can literally track your progress and see your improvements!

It's also helped you understand that life ebbs and flows. So when you are in a low, you can remember that it's not permanent. And when you're on a high you can cherish it even more. I've placed in several life wheels through this planner to help you track your progress but I highly recommend using these weekly as well!

P.s. See if you're low in a certain area don't get down on yourself! Remember if you have a 10 in everything you wouldn't need to do this! (also getting a 10 in everything all the time isn't doable! Go for those 7, 8, & 9 consistently over 10's every once and a while)

P.s.s. If you're low in all the areas ask yourself if you're being a little hard on yourself? You're allowed to give yourself a higher score and still be working on those things!

LIFE WHEEL

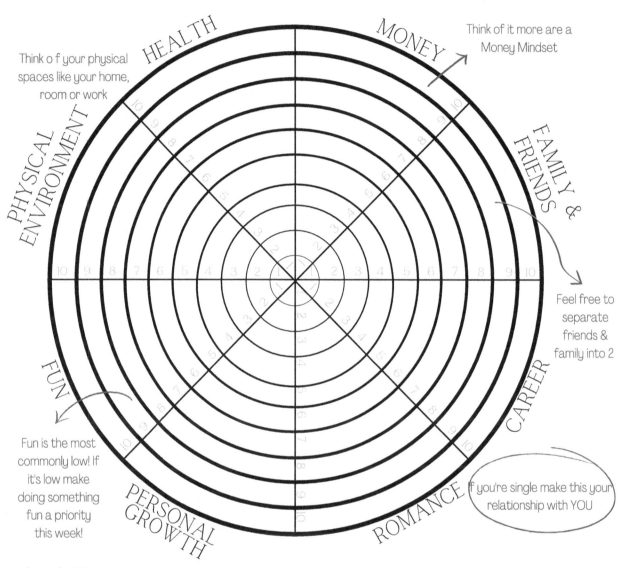

HEALTH

MONEY — Think of it more are a Money Mindset

Think o f your physical spaces like your home, room or work

PHYSICAL ENVIRONMENT

FAMILY & FRIENDS — Feel free to separate friends & family into 2

FUN — Fun is the most commonly low! If it's low make doing something fun a priority this week!

CAREER

PERSONAL GROWTH

ROMANCE — If you're single make this your relationship with YOU

1: Worse than the Worst
2: The Worst
3: It doesn't look hopeful
4: It doesn't look good
5: It looks hopeful
6: Things are okay
7: Things are going pretty good
8: Things are going good
9: It's better than I thought
10: Life is a dream

I'M PROUD I SCORED HIGHEST IN: _____
_____
_____

NOW I'M GOING TO... _____
_____
_____

TO IMPROVE... _____

LIFE WHEEL

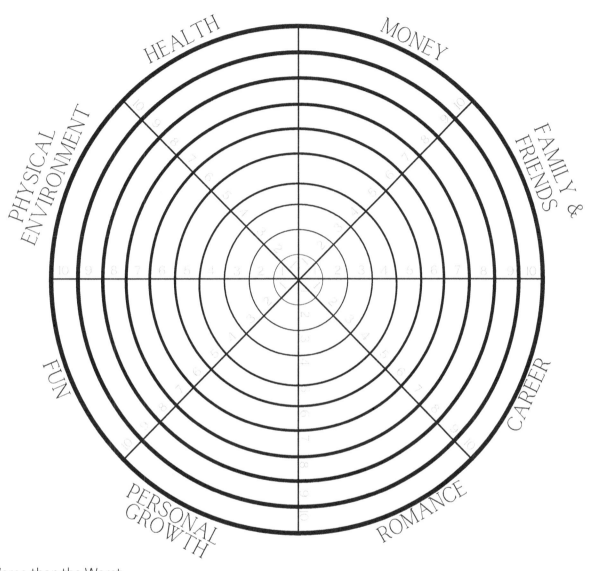

1: Worse than the Worst
2: The Worst
3: It doesn't look hopeful
4: It doesn't look good
5: It looks hopeful
6: Things are okay
7: Things are going pretty good
8: Things are going good
9: It's better than I thought
10: Life is a dream

I'M PROUD I SCORED HIGHEST IN:
_____
_____
_____

NOW I'M GOING TO...
_____
_____

TO IMPROVE...
_____

WHEN A FLOWER
DOESN'T BLOOM,
YOU FIX THE
ENVIRONMENT IN
WHICH IT GROWS
NOT THE FLOWER

WHO DO YOU REALLY WANT TO BE?

Section 1.3

Know Thyself Journal Prompts

THE JOURNAL PROMPTS

If you've done journal prompts before, they probably weren't like this! While putting thoughts and feeling into words is important, a picture can be worth a thousand words! Each journal prompt has a blank space at the bottom. Use this space to draw a picture or create a collage. If you're better with words and would rather stick with writing, I urge you to find at least one image that sums up the journal prompt.

This is going to help when we make the Action Board. *(You don't have to be into manifestation or spirituality to use an action or vision board! There's some solid science on why they work that we'll get into later)*

P.s. try to go for specific and use details when using these prompts!

WHAT I WANT TO HAVE

If you run out of space feel free to use the back side of the prompt!

Use this to add images for the prompt!

KNOW THYSELF

WHO DO I WANT TO BE

_____
_____
_____
_____
_____
_____
_____
_____
_____
_____
_____
_____

KNOW THYSELF

HOW I WANT TO LIVE

_____

_____

_____

_____

_____

_____

_____

_____

_____

_____

_____

KNOW THYSELF

WHAT I WANT TO EXPERIENCE

_____

_____

_____

_____

_____

_____

_____

_____

_____

_____

_____

KNOW THYSELF

WHAT I WANT TO HAVE

KNOW THYSELF

WHERE I SEE MYSELF IN 1 YEAR
_____

_____
_____
_____
_____
_____
_____
_____
_____
_____
_____
_____

KNOW THYSELF

WHERE I SEE MYSELF IN 3 YEAR

_____
_____
_____
_____
_____
_____
_____
_____
_____
_____
_____

KNOW THYSELF

WHERE I SEE MYSELF IN 5 YEAR

_____

_____

_____

_____

_____

_____

_____

_____

_____

KNOW THYSELF

WHY I WANT THIS LIFE
_____
_____
_____
_____
_____
_____
_____
_____
_____
_____

KNOW THYSELF

WHAT I GET FROM THIS LIFE

_____

_____

_____

_____

_____

_____

_____

_____

_____

_____

I'VE NEVER SEEN ANY LIFE TRANSFORMATION THAT DIDN'T BEGIN WITH THE PERSON FINALLY GETTING TIRED OF THEIR OWN BULLSHIT

-ELIZABETH GILBERT

BEFORE WE CONTINUE...

This section we're going over Limiting Beliefs.

Yes, I know -Why do we have to go over limiting beliefs?

Well, I'm glad you asked..

A. It's important to know what's holding you back. If you don't know this, it's not impossible to move forward. Moving forward will feel like trying to launch a ship with the anchors still down. You might get a bit off the shore, but you'll run out of steam before you can really move forward.

This leads me right to the next point...

B. Once you understand these beliefs, you can understand how to change them. Once you change your beliefs, you can start to change your life! Have you ever heard of the arrow analogy? It's when you get pulled back so you can get rocketed ahead. Working on your limiting beliefs is very much like pulling back the bow of the arrow. But once that release happens, the arrow (you) can fly forward!

C. This is probably the hardest part of the planner (in my personal opinion). So if you can make it through this you can make it through anything! Plus, I think we prove alot to ourselves when we do hard things. I want you to

Prove to Yourself You Can Do This!

IT'S LIKE A VIRUS... TOO SOON?

Section 1.4

The Virus Circle

WHAT ARE
VIRUS CIRCLES

Virus Circles are set up for you to brain dump all the limiting beliefs you can think of around a certain topic. This way your brain has space to really think about your beliefs without becoming too overwhelmed. Some main topics people tend to have limiting beliefs around are:
MONEY, RELATIONSHIP, SELF, and SITUATION.
I've laid out each one with space to fill in the beliefs that come up around it. Keep in mind some of these beliefs may overlap in certain topics. That's totally normal. Be sure to write down the same belief under each topic it comes up for!
Once you've filled in the circle, there is a quiet processing activity on the back. Jot down each belief and then select if it's true or not. Write out in what ways keeping this belief is holding you back, regardless of how true or not it may be!
P.s. I left a few virus circles blank if you wanted to add any other topics or deep dive into one particular belief!

VIRUS CIRCLES

THIS ONE IS USUALLY PRETTY EASY, WRITE OUT ALL THE LIMITING (OR NEGATIVE) BELIEFS YOU HAVE AROUND MONEY

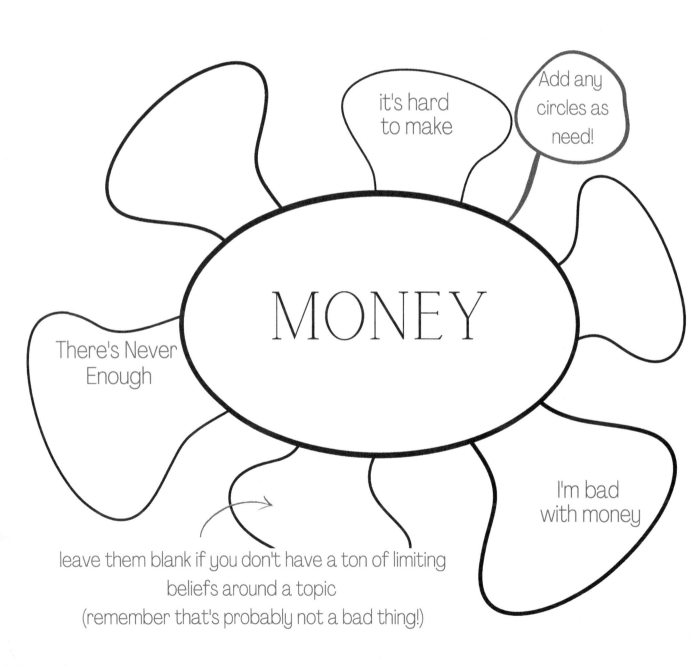

THE LIMITING BELIEF	IS THIS BELIEF TRUE	HOW IS THIS BELIEF HOLDING ME BACK
	YES - NO	
It's hard to make	No	other people make tones of money easily but I don't believe I can
There's never enough	No	There's tons of money in the World & this holds me back from seeing it!
I'm bad with money	No	Money is all about how you use it. & I want to use it for good!

VIRUS CIRCLES

THIS ONE IS USUALLY PRETTY EASY, WRITE OUT ALL THE LIMITING
(OR NEGATIVE) BELIEFS YOU HAVE AROUND MONEY

MONEY

THE LIMITING BELIEF	IS THIS BELIEF TRUE	HOW IS THIS BELIEF HOLDING ME BACK
	YES - NO	

VIRUS CIRCLES

THIS CAN BE RELATIONS WITH FAMILY, FRIENDS, A PARTNER OR FINDING A PARTNER

RELATION-SHIP

THE LIMITING BELIEF	IS THIS BELIEF TRUE	HOW IS THIS BELIEF HOLDING ME BACK
	YES - NO	

VIRUS CIRCLES

THIS ONE MAY HAVE OVERLAP FROM THE OTHERS TOPICS
YOU'VE DONE ALREADY - PUT IT HERE AGAIN

SELF

THE LIMITING BELIEF	IS THIS BELIEF TRUE	HOW IS THIS BELIEF HOLDING ME BACK
	YES - NO	

VIRUS CIRCLES

THINK OF THIS AS THE CURRENT SITUATION YOU'RE IN, JOB, LEASE, RELATIONSHIP, ETC. AND YOUR LIMITING BELIEFS AROUND IT!

SITUATION

THE LIMITING BELIEF	IS THIS BELIEF TRUE	HOW IS THIS BELIEF HOLDING ME BACK
	YES - NO	

VIRUS CIRCLES

THE LIMITING BELIEF	IS THIS BELIEF TRUE	HOW IS THIS BELIEF HOLDING ME BACK
	YES - NO	

DISCOMFORT IS THE PRICE OF ADMISSION TO A MEANINGFUL LIFE.

-SUSAN DAVIS

LIFE WHEEL

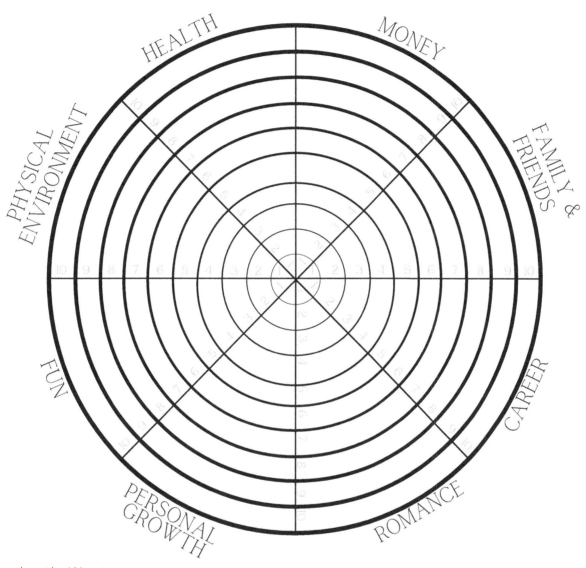

1: Worse than the Worst
2: The Worst
3: It doesn't look hopeful
4: It doesn't look good
5: It looks hopeful
6: Things are okay
7: Things are going pretty good
8: Things are going good
9: It's better than I thought
10: Life is a dream

I'M PROUD I SCORED HIGHEST IN:
_____
_____
_____

NOW I'M GOING TO...
_____
_____

TO IMPROVE...
_____

CATCH YOURSELF IN THE ACT

Section 1.5

Catch me Activity

THE CATCH ME ACTIVITY

After you finish your virus circle worksheets, there will probably be one belief that stood out to you the most. Maybe it repeated with all or alot of the different topics or it just resonated with you the most. Once you've selected your belief you can start the Catch me Activity!

This activity is pretty simple, over the next several days I want you to ask yourself - Where this belief came from? and How is it holding me back? You'll have several different prompts to help you as well.

The best thing to do is to ask yourself the prompt question in the morning and write down anything that comes up. Also, let your subconscious continue to answer the question throughout the day and take notes on what comes up. At the end of the day come back to the prompt and fill in anything else that come up throughout the day!

THE CATCH ME ACTIVITY

WHAT COMES UP WHEN I THINK OF THIS BELIEF?

_____

_____

_____

_____

_____

_____

_____

_____

_____

_____

_____

_____

_____

_____

_____

_____

_____

_____

_____

_____

_____

_____

_____

_____

THE CATCH ME ACTIVITY

HOW AM I AVOIDING SEEING, THINKING, OR HEARING THINGS THAT REMIND ME OF THIS BELIEF?

_____

_____

_____

_____

_____

_____

_____

_____

_____

_____

_____

_____

_____

_____

_____

_____

_____

_____

_____

_____

_____

_____

THE CATCH ME ACTIVITY

WHERE DID THIS BELIEF COME FROM?

THE CATCH ME ACTIVITY

WHAT MEMORIES DO I HAVE AROUND THIS BELIEF?

_____

_____

_____

_____

_____

_____

_____

_____

_____

_____

_____

_____

_____

_____

_____

_____

_____

_____

_____

_____

_____

THE CATCH ME ACTIVITY

IS THERE A PATTERN IN WHICH THIS BELIEF SHOWS UP?

_____

_____

_____

_____

_____

_____

_____

_____

_____

_____

_____

_____

_____

_____

_____

_____

_____

_____

_____

_____

_____

_____

_____

THE CATCH ME ACTIVITY

WHAT HAPPENS WHEN I LET GO OF THIS BELIEF?

THIS OR THAT
SELF CARE EDITION

HOT SHOWER	—	LONG WALK
YOGA	—	JOURNAL
MANI/PEDI	—	FACE MASK
HAVE A TREAT	—	HAVE A DRINK
PAINT/ DRAW	—	READ A BOOK
UNPLUG FROM PHONE	—	PHONE A FRIEND
TAKE A NAP	—	SLEEP IN

COMPLETE ONE DAILY AND CROSS OFF OVER THE FOLLOWING WE

AND NOW I'M GOING TO _____

Section 1.6

Fill in the Blank

FILL IN THE
BLANK

So you've identified your limiting beliefs. AND you've spent some time understanding where the belief came from, why it stuck around, and the patterns that have been keeping that belief around.
First off Round of Applause! This is no easy work but you have to till the soil before you can plant the seed. Putting in this work now helps to ensure that whatever seed you plant has a healthy space to root and grow!
This is the LAST activity we have over limiting beliefs *collective sigh of relief* This one should be pretty easy with all the work you did too!
All I want you to do is... Fill in the Blank.
This will help you really work this belief and help replace it with a new one that better serves you and the new life you're creating for yourself!

FILL IN THE BLANK

THE BELIEF   I don't have enough time

IS THIS BELIEF TRUE: YES   -   (NO)

WHAT ARE THE BENEFITS OF KEEPING THIS BELIEF AROUND?
I don't have time and never really go for it keeps me safe from
being embarrassed or putting myself out there.

I CAN'T LET   Not enough time   GO BECAUSE it keeps
me from really committing and going for it

WHAT DO I GET IF I LET THIS BELIEF GO?
I can finally start prioritizing what's important and saying no to
things that don't benefit me

IF I LET GO OF   Not enough time   I WILL   finally be able
to start the non-profit of my dreams!

NEW BELIEF   My time is my own

AFFIRMATIONS I am in control of my time
I have more than enough time to do everything need
& want to do

FILL IN THE BLANK

THE BELIEF:

_____

_____

IS THIS BELIEF TRUE: YES   -   NO

WHAT ARE THE BENEFITS OF KEEPING THIS BELIEF AROUND?

_____

_____

I CAN'T LET _____ GO BECAUSE

_____

WHAT DO I GET IF I LET THIS BELIEF GO?

_____

_____

IF I LET GO OF _____ I WILL

_____

_____

NEW BELIEF

_____

_____

_____

_____

CELEBRATION BINGO

SLEEP IN	SKIN CARE OR MOSTURIZE	HAVE A TREAT	THANK YOU LETTER TO YOURSELF	PHONE A FRIEND

10 MINUTES FOR ME	HAVE A DRINK	WATCH A SUNRISE/ SUNSET	GET DINNER DELIVERED	STAY HOME PARTY

FACEMASK/ SPA TIME	SELF DATE NIGHT	CELEB-RATE LIFE	BUY/PICK FLOWERS	HAVE A LAZY DAY

HAVE A NIGHT OUT	WATCH A MOVIE	POP BOTTLES	MANI PEDI TIME	EAT SOME CHOCOLATE

GET DRESSED UP FOR NO REASON	EAT OUT	GET A MESSAGE	PLAN A VACATION	BUY YOURSELF SOMETHING NICE

LIFE WHEEL

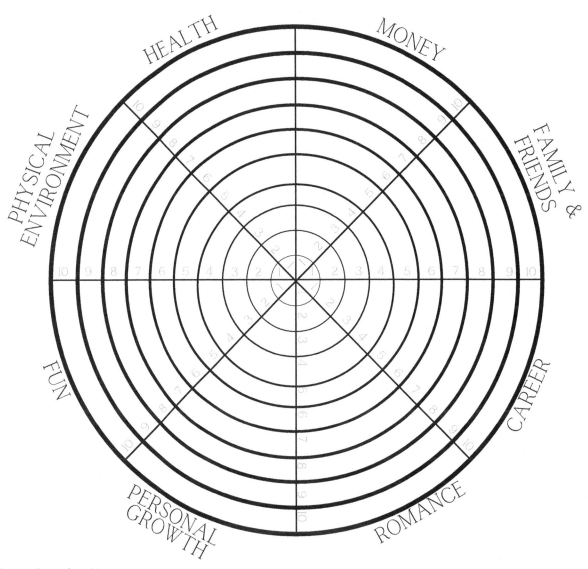

1: Worse than the Worst

2: The Worst

3: It doesn't look hopeful

4: It doesn't look good

5: It looks hopeful

6: Things are okay

7: Things are going pretty good

8: Things are going good

9: It's better than I thought

10: Life is a dream

I'M PROUD I SCORED HIGHEST IN: _____

_____

_____

NOW I'M GOING TO... _____

_____

_____

TO IMPROVE... _____

BEFORE YOU GET STARTED!

I want to give you a round of applause for making it to section two!
Section One is no easy task but you made it through.
This next section is much easier and much more fun! This section is all about
getting to know the one you are. This will help you understand who your
authentic self is- which is going to help the process of making decisions on
what you want out of your life much easier! Have fun with this section and
enjoy this time getting to know yourself a little better!

LET'S GET TO KNOW ME

Section 2.1

Ask Around Activity

WHAT IS THE ASK AROUND ACTIVITY

For this next activity, you're going to need a little help... particularly from the people who know and love you! Yep, you guessed it you're going to ask these people a few things about you! I recommend messaging people, even if you live with them or see them often. This way they have a chance to think about the answers and you can keep their message! There are 4 questions total you ask. Yes you HAVE to do this one! 😁

It's super important and will help you see things about yourself that you might usually miss. Plus it helps you understand who's really in your corner!

Pick 3 to 5 people, no more than 7 to reach out to! Once you get their responses write them down and then rewrite them in the first person. You can see the example on the next page if you're not sure how to do this!

P.s. If you're feeling insecure about asking just tell them I'm making you do it

ASK AROUND ACTIVITY

WHO I ASKED   Mom   DATE: 10 17.21

WHAT CHANGES WHEN I WALK INTO THE ROOM?
Everyone lights up and feels like they can be themselves

WHAT IS MY BIGGEST STRENGTH?
Seeing the good in others and Never letting life bring you down

WHAT'S ONE GREAT THING ABOUT ME I ALWAYS IGNORE?
How Amazing you are! and how much you have to offer the world

WHAT MAKES ME LOVABLE
Just You! The way you make life so fun and exciting!

ASK AROUND FLIPPED

WHO I ASKED   Mom   REWRITE   10.19.21

I CHANGE TH E ROOM WHEN I WALK IN BECAUSE...

I light up the room & make everyone feel like they can be themselves

MY BIGGEST STRENGTH IS...

I always see the good in others and I never let life get me down

THE GREATEST THING I ALWAYS IGNORE ABOUT MYSELF IS...

I am amazing and I have so much to offer the world

I AM LOVABLE BECAUSE...

I am loveable because I am me and I have fun and enjoy life

ASK AROUND ACTIVITY

WHO I ASKED _____ DATE: _____

WHAT CHANGES WHEN I WALK INTO THE ROOM? _____

_____

_____

_____

WHAT IS MY BIGGEST STRENGTH? _____

_____

_____

_____

WHAT'S ONE GREAT THING ABOUT ME I ALWAYS IGNORE? _____

_____

_____

_____

WHAT MAKES ME LOVABLE _____

_____

_____

_____

ASK AROUND FLIPPED

WHO I ASKED   REWRITE:
_____   _____

I CHANGE THE ROOM WHEN I WALK IN BECAUSE...
_____
_____
_____
_____

MY BIGGEST STRENGTH IS...
_____
_____
_____
_____

THE GREATEST THING I ALWAYS IGNORE ABOUT MYSELF IS...
_____
_____
_____
_____

I AM LOVABLE BECAUSE...
_____
_____
_____
_____

ASK AROUND ACTIVITY

WHO I ASKED _____ DATE: _____

WHAT CHANGES WHEN I WALK INTO THE ROOM? _____
_____
_____
_____

WHAT IS MY BIGGEST STRENGTH? _____
_____
_____
_____

WHAT'S ONE GREAT THING ABOUT ME I ALWAYS IGNORE? ____
_____
_____
_____

WHAT MAKES ME LOVABLE _____
_____
_____
_____

ASK AROUND FLIPPED

WHO I ASKED   REWRITE:
_____   _____

I CHANGE THE ROOM WHEN I WALK IN BECAUSE...
_____
_____
_____
_____

MY BIGGEST STRENGTH IS...
_____
_____
_____
_____

THE GREATEST THING I ALWAYS IGNORE ABOUT MYSELF IS...
_____
_____
_____
_____

I AM LOVABLE BECAUSE...
_____
_____
_____
_____

ASK AROUND ACTIVITY

WHO I ASKED _____ DATE: _____

WHAT CHANGES WHEN I WALK INTO THE ROOM? _____
_____
_____
_____

WHAT IS MY BIGGEST STRENGTH? _____
_____
_____
_____

WHAT'S ONE GREAT THING ABOUT ME I ALWAYS IGNORE? _____
_____
_____
_____

WHAT MAKES ME LOVABLE _____
_____
_____
_____

ASK AROUND FLIPPED

WHO I ASKED _____ REWRITE: _____

I CHANGE THE ROOM WHEN I WALK IN BECAUSE...
_____
_____
_____
_____

MY BIGGEST STRENGTH IS...
_____
_____
_____
_____

THE GREATEST THING I ALWAYS IGNORE ABOUT MYSELF IS...
_____
_____
_____
_____

I AM LOVABLE BECAUSE...
_____
_____
_____
_____

YOU EITHER WALK INSIDE
YOUR STORY AND OWN
IT OR YOU STAND
OUTSIDE YOUR STORY
AND HUSTLE FOR YOUR
WORTHINESS.

-BRENE BROWN

AND THE ANSWER SAYS... I'M ME

Section 2.2
Personality Tests

PERSONALITY TESTS

This is probably the most fun section! Each test is going to tell you a little bit more about who you are and what you're amazing at!
Try not to do them all at once, shoot for no more than one a day or move at a pace that works best for you! Just don't rush it!

- The 16 Personality Test: this is going to give you a great overview and deep dive into your personality - Warning this can be spookily accurate! You can take the test by going to https://www.16personalities.com

- The Enneagram Personality Test: this is going to give you numbers that will help line up with your personality and how they interact with other personality types! You can take your enneagram test free at https://www.truity.com/test/enneagram-personality-test

BE IN A CONSTANT STATE OF SELF-IMPROVEMENT BUT DON'T BEAT YOURSELF UP OVER IT.

LET'S MAP THINGS OUT

Section 2.3

Me Mind Map

WHAT IS THE
ME MIND MAP

A mind map is a space to brain dump, and a Me Mind Map is a space to brain dump everything about you!

I've given you prompts around different topics and a blank one to fill in freely. Add as many additional combs to your map as you see it! You also have the added bonus of adding a visual in the center of your mind map. This can be a drawing as a self-portrait or a photograph. Feel free to get creative with it and have fun finding an image that represents you or the topic of your mind map!

ME MIND MAP

Self

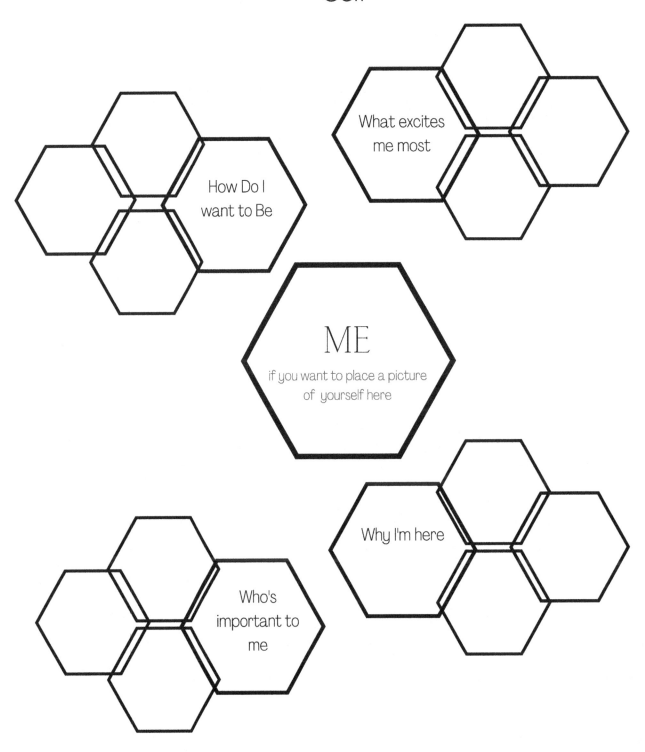

How Do I want to Be

What excites me most

ME

if you want to place a picture of yourself here

Who's important to me

Why I'm here

ME MIND MAP

Relationship

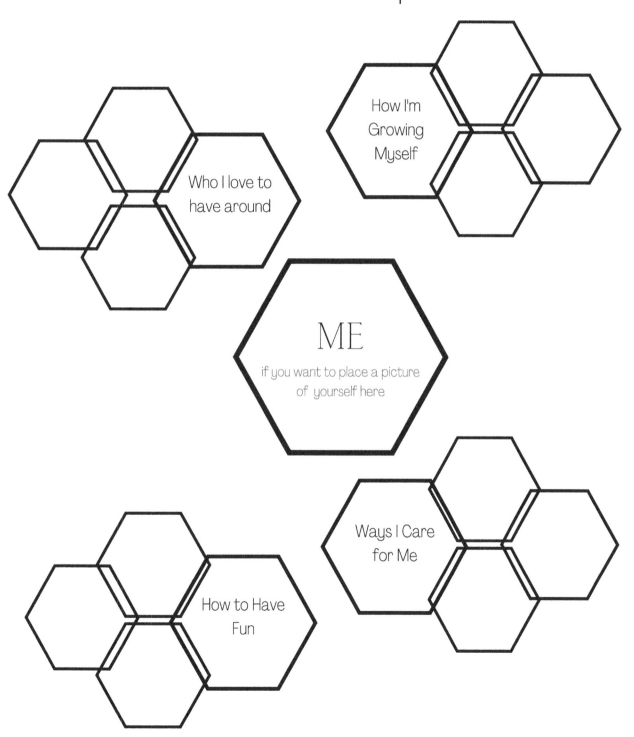

How I'm Growing Myself

Who I love to have around

ME

if you want to place a picture of yourself here

Ways I Care for Me

How to Have Fun

ME MIND MAP

Money/ Career

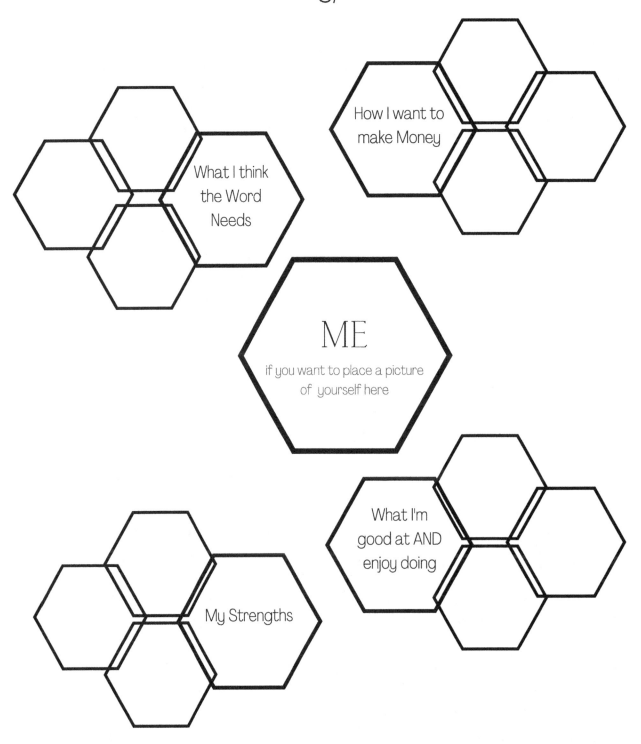

How I want to make Money

What I think the Word Needs

ME

if you want to place a picture of yourself here

What I'm good at AND enjoy doing

My Strengths

ME MIND MAP

ME

if you want to place a picture
of yourself here

YOU HAVE SO MUCH TO OFFER AS THE PERSON YOU ARE RIGHT NOW

I'M GOOD AT LOTS OF THINGS

Section 2.4

Good at Prompts

THE GOOD AT PROMPTS

This Prompt is very similar to the ones we used in Section One for the 'Know Thy Self Prompt'. There will be a section for you to write, doodle, or place images. Feel free to use this space as you find needed! It's not as important to find pictures with this prompt so you can also use it for an overflow of the writing section!

As always take your time completing these prompts. Try not to complete more than one a day; but remember, you're a human being who probably has a busy life. So if you miss a day or two just pick up where you left off!

GOOD AT PROMPTS

WHAT SKILLS HAVE HELPED ME THRIVE?

_____

_____

_____

_____

_____

_____

_____

_____

_____

_____

GOOD AT PROMPTS

WHAT MAKES ME FEEL STRONG?

_____
_____
_____
_____
_____
_____
_____
_____
_____
_____
_____

GOOD AT PROMPTS

WHAT COMPLIMENTS DO I IGNORE?

_____
_____
_____
_____
_____
_____
_____
_____
_____
_____

GOOD AT PROMPTS

WHAT MADE ME STAND OUT WHEN I WAS YOUNGER?

_____

_____

_____

_____

_____

_____

_____

_____

_____

_____

GOOD AT PROMPTS

WHAT DO I ENJOY DOING THAT HELPS OTHERS?

_____
_____
_____
_____
_____
_____
_____
_____
_____
_____

FIND OUT WHO YOU ARE AND DO IT ON PURPOSE.

-DOLLY PARTON

BUT WHAT'S THE PURPOSE?

Section 2.5
Purpose Circles

WHAT ARE PURPOSE CIRCLES?

Purpose Circles, also known as Ikigai Circles, best translates to the reason you get up in the morning. It's a great way to think about your purpose. Some may call it their Why, or their reason for being, but whatever you call it. It's important to understand your purpose may not be one thing. It will very likely change over time. So allow space for that to happen! And don't get caught up trying to find one thing to be your purpose. The goal is to realize the purpose in all the little things throughout your day. This will truly be the first step to leading a Purpose filled life!

PURPOSE CIRCLES

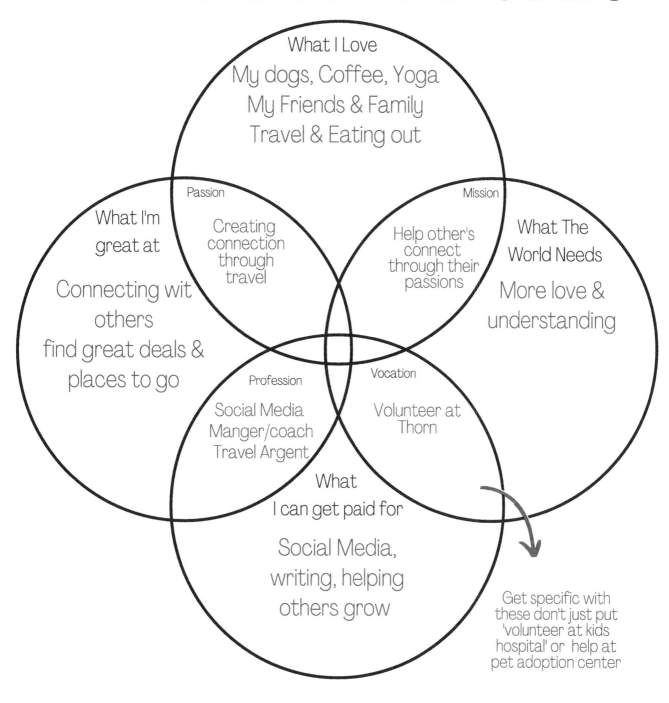

What I Love
My dogs, Coffee, Yoga
My Friends & Family
Travel & Eating out

Passion
Creating connection through travel

Mission
Help other's connect through their passions

What I'm great at
Connecting wit others
find great deals & places to go

What The World Needs
More love & understanding

Profession
Social Media Manger/coach
Travel Argent

Vocation
Volunteer at Thorn

What I can get paid for
Social Media, writing, helping others grow

Get specific with these don't just put 'volunteer at kids hospital' or help at pet adoption center

MY PURPOSE: Create meaningful connections

PURPOSE CIRCLES

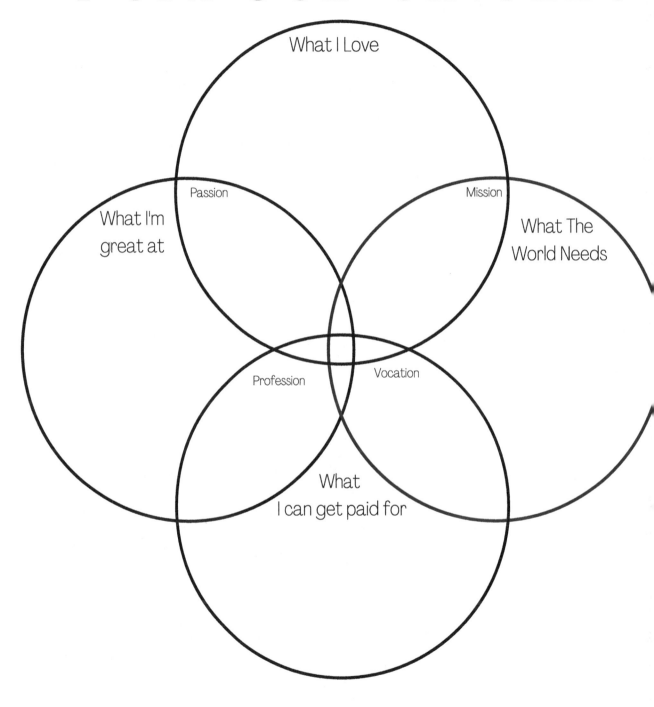

What I Love

Passion

Mission

What I'm great at

What The World Needs

Profession

Vocation

What I can get paid for

MY PURPOSE: _____

SELF CARE BINGO

BUBBLE BATH (OR HOT SHOWER) 	MANI PEDI TIME 	PHONE A FRIEND 	TAKE A WALK 	MEDITATE 
TAKE A NAP 	HYDRATE 	READ 	COOK A NEW MEAL 	FACEMASK/ SPA TIME 
UNPLUG 	SLEEP IN 	STAY ALIVE 	WATCH A MOVIE 	HAVE A TREAT 
JAM TO SOME TUNES 	YOGA/ STRETCH 	WORK OUT 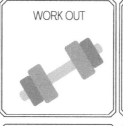	DRAWER OR PAINT 	HAVE A DRINK 
GET SOME SUN 	SKIN CARE OR MOSTURIZE 	COFFEE OR TEA 	JOURNAL 	1 MINUTE DEEP BREATHING 

LIFE WHEEL

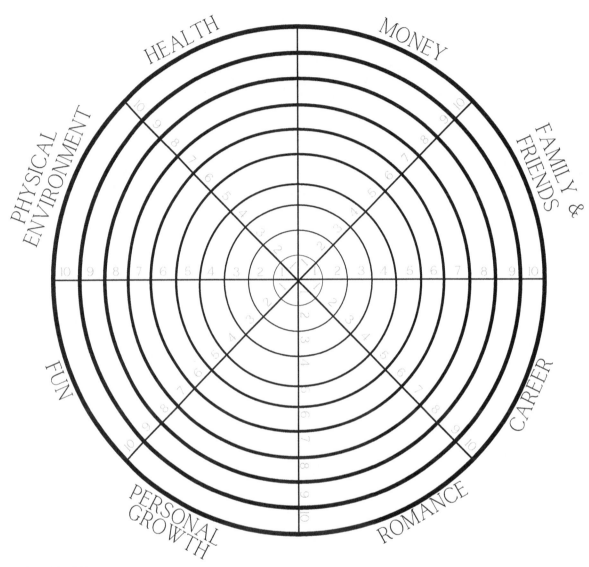

1: Worse than the Worst
2: The Worst
3: It doesn't look hopeful
4: It doesn't look good
5: It looks hopeful
6: Things are okay
7: Things are going pretty good
8: Things are going good
9: It's better than I thought
10: Life is a dream

I'M PROUD I SCORED HIGHEST IN: _____
_____
_____

NOW I'M GOING TO... _____
_____

TO IMPROVE... _____

WHY ARE WE DOING THIS AGAIN

Section 2.6

Why Statement

WHAT IS A 'WHY' STATEMENT?

A 'Why' Statement is one of *the most life changing* things you are going to do in this planner! It's also one of the hardest things you're going to do. Not necessarily because it's difficult but because it requires a deep level of thought into why you are doing what you do.

Your 'Why' Statement should be around 1 to 3 sentences. I've given you prompts to help guide you on how to create your 'Why' Statement! You also have an example so use that as a reference! After you created your 'Why' Statement please, please PLEASE start writing it every day. Write one out large enough and place it somewhere you can read it every day! Just like your purpose, your 'Why' statement will change over time. Don't be afraid to make it all about you! Don't be afraid to make it broad! Don't be afraid to change and edit it as many times as you see fit!

WHY STATEMENT

WHAT DRIVES ME TO KEEP GOING EVERYDAY?

Feeling like I could help

make a difference in

someone's life that

makes a ripple-effect

of positivity

WHAT DO I WANT PEOPLE TO TAKE AWAY FROM OUR INTERACTIONS

A feeling that they are

here for a reason and

can accomplish

anything!

WHAT DO I NOT WANT REGRET FROM LIFE?

I don't want to look back.

and feel like I never went

for it.

MY WHY STATEMENT

Live my biggest fullest most authentic life

- or -

Live my biggest fullest most authentic life & help inspire/guide
others to do the same

WHY STATEMENT

WHAT DRIVES ME TO KEEP GOING EVERYDAY?

_____
_____
_____
_____
_____
_____
_____
_____
_____
_____
_____
_____
_____
_____
_____
_____
_____

WHAT DO I WANT PEOPLE TO TAKE AWAY FROM OUR INTERACTIONS

_____
_____
_____
_____
_____
_____
_____
_____
_____
_____
_____
_____
_____
_____
_____
_____
_____

WHAT DO I NOT WANT REGRET FROM LIFE?

_____
_____
_____
_____
_____
_____
_____
_____
_____
_____
_____
_____
_____
_____
_____
_____
_____

MY WHY STATEMENT

_____
_____
_____
_____
_____
_____

THIS OR THAT
CELEBRATION EDITION

DO NOTHING DAY   —   SELF DATE NIGHT

MANI/PEDI   —   FACIAL

HAVE A TREAT   —   HAVE A DRINK

WATCH THE SUNRISE   —   WATCH THE SUNSET

EAT OUT   —   HAVE FOOD DELIVERED

BUY FLOWERS   —   BUY CHOCOLATE

GO OUT   —   PARTY AT HOME

COMPLETE ONE DAILY AND CROSS OFF OVER THE FOLLOWING WE

BEFORE YOU MOVE ON...

This is our last workbook section. After this, you're actually getting... A PLANNER! (I know right?! finally) Really milk this last section for all its worth! This is going to be the deep dive into what you really want from this life so you can proceed forward to making a plan for it!

Trust me when I say all this work is going to help make the plan and the execution better. I'm not going to lie to you and tell you it makes it easier because it will still be hard at times, but when you do this work, and you understand what's holding you back - who you really are, and what you really want out of life. You will be unstoppable!

A 'DREAM'
DAY
IN THE LIFE

Section 3.1

Dream Day Activity

WHAT IS THE DREAM DAY ACTIVITY?

The Dream Day Activity is so simple yet so important! We all have a vague idea of what a day in our dream life would look like... but do you really know the details of that day? Do you really have a clear vision of what that day looks like from start to finish?

This activity is going to help you work out all those details!

DREAM DAY
ACTIVITY

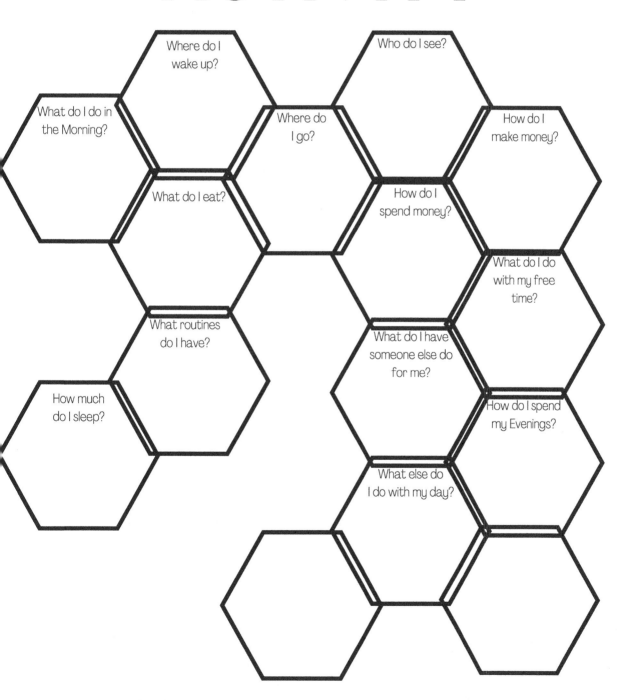

Where do I wake up?

Who do I see?

What do I do in the Morning?

Where do I go?

How do I make money?

What do I eat?

How do I spend money?

What do I do with my free time?

What routines do I have?

What do I have someone else do for me?

How much do I sleep?

How do I spend my Evenings?

What else do I do with my day?

DREAM DAY

MY DREAM DAY FROM START TO FINISH

5 AM

6 AM

7 AM

8 AM

9 AM

10 AM

11 AM

12 PM

1 PM

2 PM

3 PM

4 PM

5 PM

6 PM

7 PM

8 PM

9 PM

10 PM

11 PM

12 AM

1 AM

2 AM

3 AM

4 AM

DREAM DAY

DREAM DAY VISUALS

WHAT'S SOMETHING FROM MY
DREAM DAY I CAN START DOING NOW?

_____
_____
_____
_____

I DO NOT CHASE,
I AM ATTACHED.
WHAT BELONGS TO
ME WILL SIMPLY
FIND ME.

THE MAP
TO MY
DREAMS

Section 3.2
Dream Mapping

WHAT IS DREAM MAPPING?

Dream Mapping also know as 'Dreamlining' from Tim Ferris' Book, *The 4 Hour Work Week*, is going to get into the nitty-gritty of just how much this dream life of yours is going to cost you! You are going to discover several things doing this activity:

a. Becoming who you want to 'be' almost always costs very little, if any money at all, and will have the biggest impact on your life

b. There will be experiences on your list that are much cheaper than you expected. Please, for the love of all that is good pick one and do it in the next 30 days. Prove to yourself that you're the kind of person who does the things they want to do in life!

c. Apart from your dream house and your dream car(s) and maybe one or two other things, most things are probably not going to be as much as you thought! For the big items figure out your down payment and start saving toward it monthly. For your smaller items, just like with your experiences, pick one that is doable and make a plan to purchase it in the next month!

P.s. Be as specific as you can! This is going to help when finding the cost of things

DREAM MAP

COST/COST TYPE

BEING

	Monthly	One Time
Learn French	Free	
Learn to Cook	Free	+ supplies
Start a Garden	Free	+ supplies

I WILL START...

Learn French by downloading a learning app like Babbel

BY DATE: Today!

DOING

	Monthly	One Time
Paragliding		$115
Backpack thru Europe		$3724
Go to Yellowstone		$732

I WILL DO...

I Will go Paragliding with my next paycheck

BY DATE: in 2 weeks

HAVING

	Monthly	One Time
Cannon Rebel Camera		$300
Tesla	$400	$5400
My Own House	$1800	$12,000

I WILL BUY...

I will save $100 a a month to buy my

Cannon Rebel

BY DATE: Monthly

Total Monthly: $2200   Total One Time: $21,671

DREAM MAP

COST/COST TYPE

BEING		
	Monthly	One Time
_____	_____	_____
_____	_____	_____
_____	_____	_____
_____	_____	_____
_____	_____	_____
_____	_____	_____

I WILL START...

_____
_____
_____
_____
_____
_____

BY DATE:

DOING		
	Monthly	One Time
_____	_____	_____
_____	_____	_____
_____	_____	_____
_____	_____	_____
_____	_____	_____
_____	_____	_____

I WILL DO...

_____
_____
_____
_____
_____
_____

BY DATE:

HAVING		
	Monthly	One Time
_____	_____	_____
_____	_____	_____
_____	_____	_____
_____	_____	_____
_____	_____	_____
_____	_____	_____

I WILL BUY...

_____
_____
_____
_____
_____
_____

BY DATE:

Total Monthly: _____

Total One Time: _____

YOU DON'T JUST WAKE UP AND BECOME THE BUTTERFLY GROWTH IS A PROCESS

CAN YOU ENVISION IT?

Section 3.3

Action Board

HOW TO DO AN ACTION BOARD

An Action Board, also known as, a Dream or Vision board is going to be a visional collage of everything you aspire to be. It is set up from the steps used by Tara Swart, a neuroscientist and former psychiatric doctor turned into Life Improvement coach and author of the book 'The Source.' This activity works so well with manifestation by priming the brain to see opportunities that can make these visualization happen. Think of Manifesting like a 401k plan that your employer matches. You still have to put money in, but the more you put in the more you get in return. The Universe works the same way with manifestation!

P.s This is not for your daydreams of homes and vacations. This is a collage of images that represent who you want to be and the life you want to live

ACTION BOARD STEPS:

1. Spend at least one week on this activity! This is going to be your Action Board for the next 12 to 18 months so you don't want to rush it!

2. Use little to No words! If you choose to, use only one word or phrase! If you are manifesting a certain amount of money, be sure to put the exact amount of money on your action board!

3. Gather as many images as you can! When you think you have enough images, gather more! And be sure to use images metaphorically. For example- *if you're moving you can put in images of a home, but you can also use a balloon to represent the freedom that the move will bring!*

4. Once you've spent a few days gathering images and place them on your board. Be conscious of how you're placing your images
   a. Keep the most important images at the top or in the center
   b. Group images together based on what they represent
   c. Decide if you want the images to overlap like a collage. If you want more space in your life be sure to not clutter your board
   d. After you've laid out the images wait 24 hours before coming back and making edits. Remove images that don't feel right, and go back to your original pile of images to see if you want to add anything else
   e. After you complete this place your vision board somewhere you will see it EVERY DAY! *(Pro Tip: Take Picture of Your Action Board and Use it as Your Screen Saver!)*

ACTION BOARD

NO MORE WAITING TO BECOME.
IT'S TIME TO SIMPLY BE

IT ALL HAS TO START SOMEWHERE

Section 3.4

Where I am Activity

WHAT IS THE WHERE I AM ACTIVITY?

So often we can feel like we are at the bottom of a mountain and we see that where we want to be is so far away at the top. And we're stuck wearing flip-flops. Not only do we have no idea where to start but we feel super unprepared! This activity is going to help you map out the steps you need, and what actions you need to take to make to make those steps possible. This is a rinse and repeat method. When you finish your first step you can come back and redo this activity for the next step you've mapped out!

P.s. I have mapped out 4 steps - feel free to add as mare steps or use fewer steps as needed!

WHERE I AM

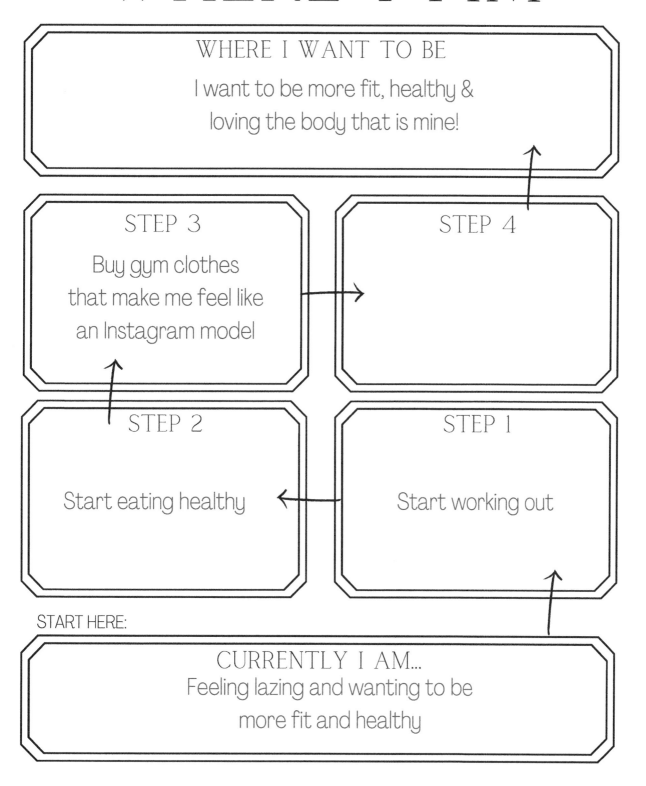

WHERE I WANT TO BE
I want to be more fit, healthy &
loving the body that is mine!

STEP 3
Buy gym clothes
that make me feel like
an Instagram model

STEP 4

STEP 2
Start eating healthy

STEP 1
Start working out

START HERE:

CURRENTLY I AM...
Feeling lazing and wanting to be
more fit and healthy

WHERE I AM

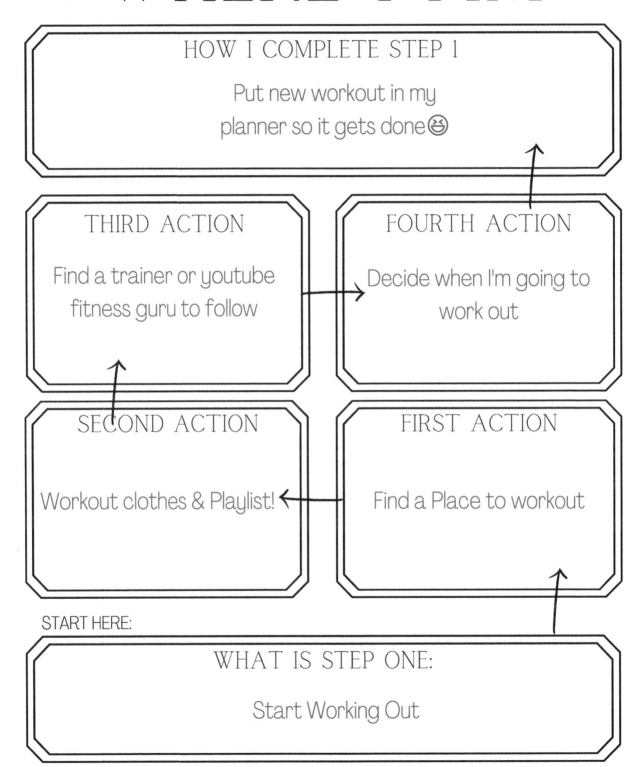

HOW I COMPLETE STEP 1

Put new workout in my
planner so it gets done😆

THIRD ACTION

Find a trainer or youtube
fitness guru to follow

FOURTH ACTION

Decide when I'm going to
work out

SECOND ACTION

Workout clothes & Playlist!

FIRST ACTION

Find a Place to workout

START HERE:

WHAT IS STEP ONE:

Start Working Out

WHERE I AM

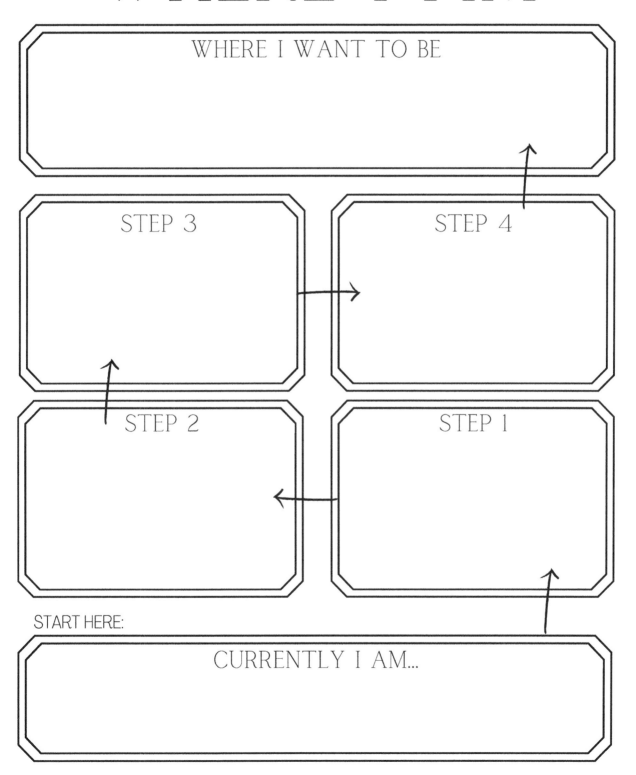

WHERE I WANT TO BE

STEP 3

STEP 4

STEP 2

STEP 1

START HERE:

CURRENTLY I AM...

WHERE I AM

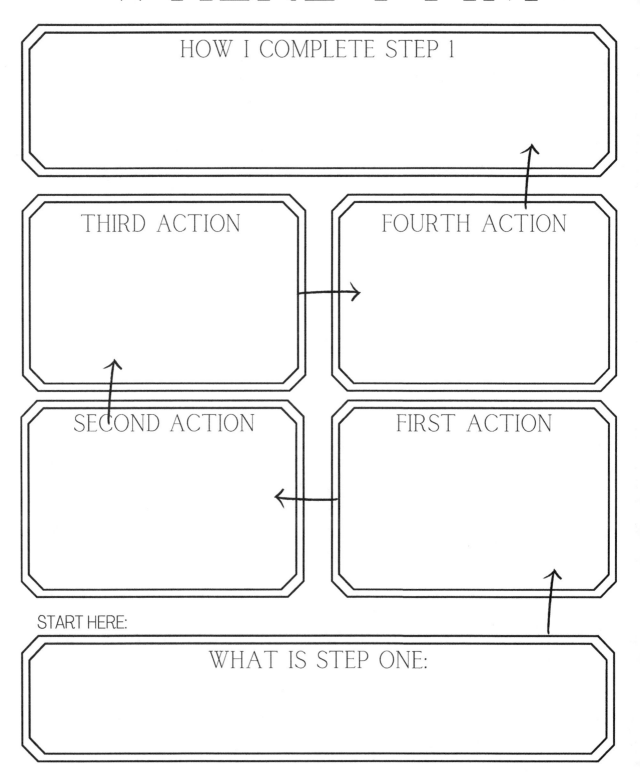

HOW I COMPLETE STEP 1

THIRD ACTION

FOURTH ACTION

SECOND ACTION

FIRST ACTION

START HERE:

WHAT IS STEP ONE:

WHAT WE FEAR
DOING MOST IS
USUALLY WHAT
WE MOST NEED
TO DO.

-TIM FERRIS

DO IT

SCARED,

TRUST ME

Section 3.5

Fear Setting

HOW TO DO A FEAR SETTING

Fear Setting is an amazing trick I first heard about from entrepreneur and author, and lifestyle guru Tim Ferris. This is a lot like working backward. It's going to help you understand your Fears around something rather than why you want that thing. This is so important when deciding what you're doing because oftentimes when unknown fears come up we get stopped in our tracks. This will help you identify these fears and how to deal with them before you even start the journey - giving you even more confidence and motivation!

FEAR SETTING

WHAT IS MY FEAR?

Starting My Own Business

BRAIN DUMP ALL THE FEARS AROUND THIS

I'll run out of money
I can't go back to work

HOW CAN I PREVENT THIS?

Cut back on costs
Find freelance jobs

IF IT HAPPENS HOW CAN I FIX IT?

Save money
Find a new job

THE BENEFIT FROM JUST ATTEMPTING?

Can learn new skills
that can help me
with my later
careers

THE BENEFIT FROM PARTIAL SUCCESS?

I learn that I'm the
Person that can run
my own Business

THE BENEFIT FROM FULL BLOWN SUCCESS?

I Will have the
success business of
my dreams and be
super proud of myself

WHAT HAPPENS IN 6 MONTHS IF I DO NOTHING?

I have to stay in the
job I'll hate and
watch other people
go for their dreams

WHAT HAPPENS IN 1 YEAR IF I DO NOTHING?

I'm still at my job, I have
no clear idea of how life
is going to get any
better from here..

WHAT HAPPENS IN 3 YEARS IF I DO NOTHING?

My business feels even
harder to start and I
feel even more stuck
then even, meaning I
may never go for it!

FEAR SETTING

WHAT IS MY FEAR?

_____
_____

BRAIN DUMP ALL THE FEARS AROUND THIS

_____
_____
_____
_____
_____

HOW CAN I PREVENT THIS?

_____
_____
_____
_____
_____

IF IT HAPPENS HOW CAN I FIX IT?

_____
_____
_____
_____
_____

THE BENEFIT FROM JUST ATTEMPTING?

_____
_____
_____
_____
_____

THE BENEFIT FROM PARTIAL SUCCESS?

_____
_____
_____
_____
_____

THE BENEFIT FROM FULL BLOWN SUCCESS?

_____
_____
_____
_____
_____

WHAT HAPPENS IN 6 MONTHS IF I DO NOTHING?

_____
_____
_____
_____
_____

WHAT HAPPENS IN 1 YEAR IF I DO NOTHING?

_____
_____
_____
_____
_____

WHAT HAPPENS IN 3 YEARS IF I DO NOTHING?

_____
_____
_____
_____
_____

FEAR SETTING

WHAT IS MY FEAR?

_____
_____

BRAIN DUMP ALL THE FEARS AROUND THIS

_____
_____
_____
_____
_____

HOW CAN I PREVENT THIS?

_____
_____
_____
_____
_____

IF IT HAPPENS HOW CAN I FIX IT?

_____
_____
_____
_____
_____

THE BENEFIT FROM JUST ATTEMPTING?

_____
_____
_____
_____
_____

THE BENEFIT FROM PARTIAL SUCCESS?

_____
_____
_____
_____
_____

THE BENEFIT FROM FULL BLOWN SUCCESS?

_____
_____
_____
_____
_____

WHAT HAPPENS IN 6 MONTHS IF I DO NOTHING?

_____
_____
_____
_____
_____

WHAT HAPPENS IN 1 YEAR IF I DO NOTHING?

_____
_____
_____
_____
_____

WHAT HAPPENS IN 3 YEARS IF I DO NOTHING?

_____
_____
_____
_____
_____

LIFE WHEEL

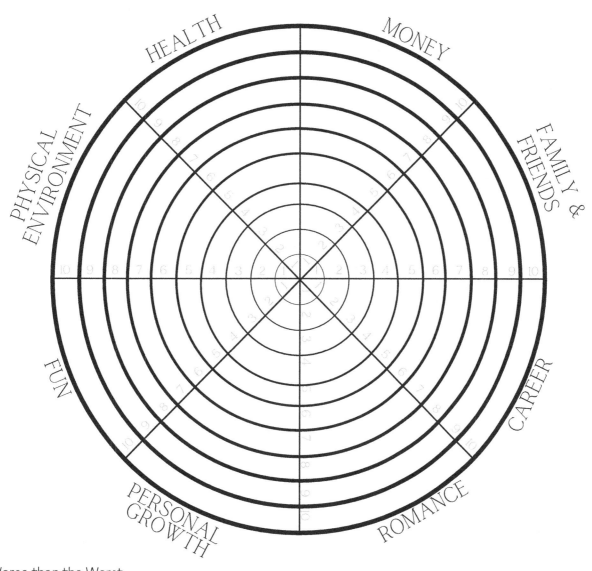

1: Worse than the Worst
2: The Worst
3: It doesn't look hopeful
4: It doesn't look good
5: It looks hopeful
6: Things are okay
7: Things are going pretty good
8: Things are going good
9: It's better than I thought
10: Life is a dream

I'M PROUD I SCORED HIGHEST IN:
_____
_____
_____

NOW I'M GOING TO...
_____
_____
_____

TO IMPROVE...
_____

THIS OR THAT
SELF CARE EDITION

COOK A NEW MEAL   —   EAT SOMEWHERE NEW

WORKOUT   —   MEDITATE

NO ALCHOLE   —   NO PHONE

GET OUTSIDE   —   MAKE A DIY

GO TO BED EARLY   —   TAKE A LONG LUNCH

GO OUT WIHT FRIENDS   —   HAVE A SPA NIGHT IN

DO HAIR   —   DO NAILS

COMPLETE ONE DAILY AND CROSS OFF OVER THE
FOLLOWING WEEK

PICK YOUR HARD

Section 3.6
If I Change

IF I CHANGE JOURNAL PROMTS

I need to get real with you for a minute...Changing your life is hard, but so is
staying in the same life you hate.
Pick your hard- because whether you like it or not, it is a choice.
To Finish up this Section, take some time to complete these prompts.
Always feel free to use any images that feel appropriate!

IF I CHANGE...

WHAT DO I WANT TO CHANGE

_____

_____

_____

_____

_____

_____

_____

_____

_____

_____

IF I CHANGE...

WHAT DO I GET FROM CHANGING?

_____
_____
_____
_____
_____
_____
_____
_____
_____
_____

IF I CHANGE...

WHAT WILL BE TH HARDEST PART OF CHANGING?

_____

_____

_____

_____

_____

_____

_____

_____

_____

_____

IF I CHANGE...

HOW DOES CHANGING CHANGE ME?

_____
_____
_____
_____
_____
_____
_____
_____
_____
_____
_____

IF I CHANGE...

WHAT HAPPENS AFTER I CHANGE

_____

_____

_____

_____

_____

_____

_____

_____

_____

_____

IF I CHANGE...

WHAT HAPPENS IF I DON'T CHANGE?

_____

_____

_____

_____

_____

_____

_____

_____

_____

_____

THIS OR THAT
CELEBRATION EDITION

DO NOTHING DAY — SELF DATE NIGHT

MANI/PEDI — FACIAL

HAVE A TREAT — HAVE A DRINK

WATCH THE SUNRISE — WATCH THE SUNSET

EAT OUT — HAVE FOOD DELIVERED

BUY FLOWERS — BUY CHOCOLATE

GO OUT — PARTY AT HOME

COMPLETE ONE DAILY AND CROSS OFF
OVER THE FOLLOWING WE

LET'S GET READY TO DO THIS

You have done so much work. Please make sure you take time to celebrate before moving into your last section! This section will have a few more activities and then we'll finally get to the planner part of it already! Just know if you're reading this I am SO truly and deeply proud of you for doing this work!

DECISIONS, DECISIONS...

Section 4.1

Decision Circles

HOW TO DO DECISION CIRCLES

Decision Circles are going to be the last activity we get into the planner!
(I know I said we were done after that last section, I lied)
This is going to help you really decide what direction you want to go in with your life. And while the planner will have guided steps for you to help your succees it's still important to know what your target is!
Your Decision Circles work from the inside out; if you can't answer the first question then go to Sections Two & Three.

DECISION CIRCLES

WHAT IS THE DECISION
Should I go to for the Job of my Dreams Over the Job
that Mkes me a ton of money

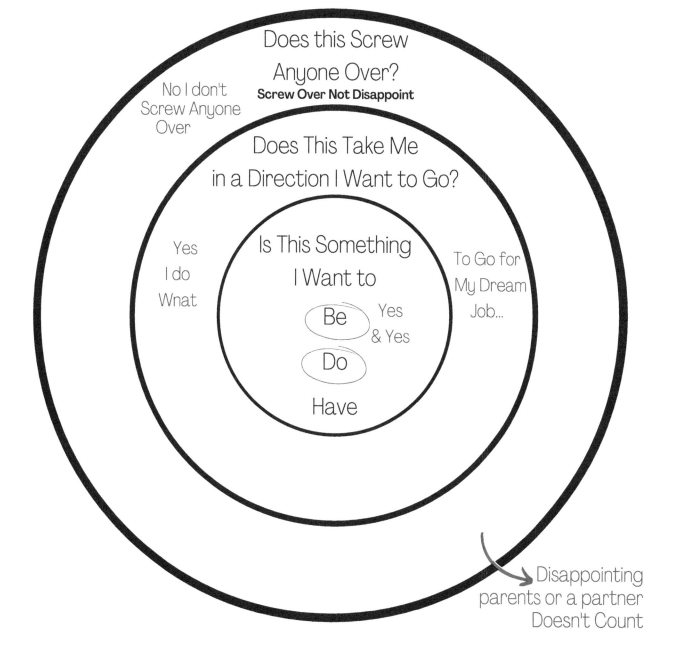

Does this Screw Anyone Over?
Screw Over Not Disappoint

No I don't Screw Anyone Over

Does This Take Me in a Direction I Want to Go?

Yes I do Wnat

Is This Something I Want to

Be — Yes & Yes

Do

To Go for My Dream Job...

Have

Disappointing parents or a partner Doesn't Count

DECISION CIRCLES

WHAT IS THE DECISION

_____
_____
_____

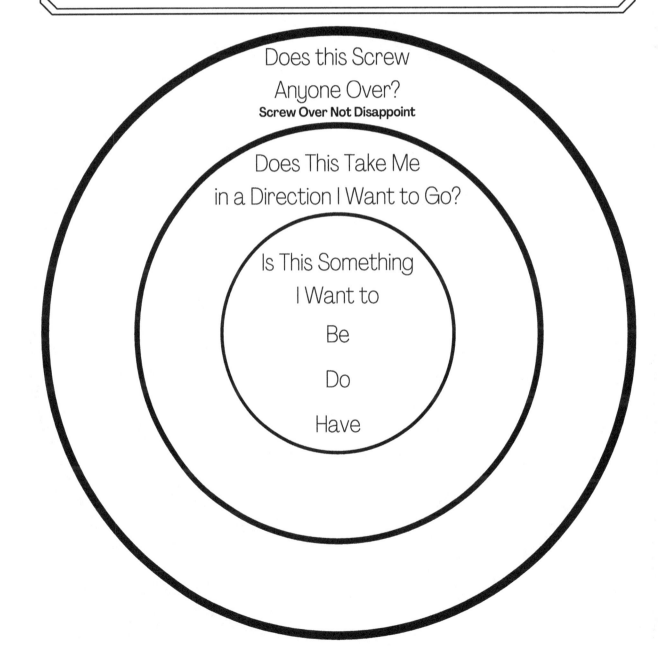

Does this Screw
Anyone Over?
Screw Over Not Disappoint

Does This Take Me
in a Direction I Want to Go?

Is This Something
I Want to

Be

Do

Have

SO OFTEN, WE
PRETEND WE'VE
MADE A DECISION
WHEN WHAT WE'VE
REALLY DONE IS
SIGNED UP TO TRY
UNTIL IT GETS TOO
UNCOMFORTABLE.

-JEN SINCERO

LIFE WHEEL

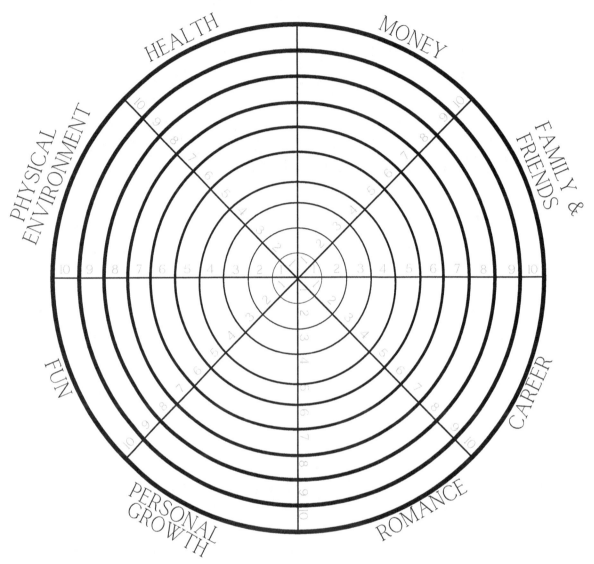

1: Worse than the Worst
2: The Worst
3: It doesn't look hopeful
4: It doesn't look good
5: It looks hopeful
6: Things are okay
7: Things are going pretty good
8: Things are going good
9: It's better than I thought
10: Life is a dream

I'M PROUD I SCORED HIGHEST IN: _____
_____
_____

NOW I'M GOING TO... _____
_____
_____

TO IMPROVE... _____

YOU HAVE ARRIVED

Section 4.2

Monthly Planner

HOW TO SET UP THE MONTHLY PLANNER

The Monthly Planner is set up for you to fill in every month. The Most unique thing about the Monthly Planner is the THREE big goals you set! Theses Goals will Be Key Moving Forward with the Weekly and Daily Planner. One Goal will already be filled out for you to help you get started. If you still need help, start small and think of the first step you need to take to reach your goal! (Found in Section 3.4)

The Monthly Check-in Will be Done at the end of the month!

P.s. If you can only come up with one goal that's totally okay! It's always better to start small and have success than to start too large - get overwhelmed and give up!

Put Month Here

SUN	MON	TUE	WED	THRU	FRI	SAT
1	2	3	4	Fill in days		

One Goal Will Already Be Filled Out for to help get you Started

GOAL GETTER

☐ START USING PLANER

☐ Start Morning Routine

☐ _____

THE WAY TO GET STARTED IS TO QUIT TALKING AND BEGIN DOING.

Walt Disney

IMPORTANT DATES

MONTHYLY RECAP

I'M PROUDEST OF MYSELF FOR

Trying my best to keep using my planner
when I skipped a few days

I'M SO BRAVE FOR

Leaving my friends earlier than everyone else so I could get
up and do my morning routine!

THE HARDEST THING I DID

Making Myself a Bed time!

MY FAVORITE MEMORY

Dinner and games with my family no feeling bad or like there
was something else I needed to be

YOU WILL FACE MANY DEFEATS IN YOUR LIFE,
BUT NEVER LET YURELF BE DEFEATED.

MAYA ANGELOU

I'VE GOT BIG PLANS

Start Planning Girls Trip!!!

IMPORTANT
DATES NEXT
MONTH

Grandma's
Birthday!

SUN	MON	TUE	WED	THRU	FRI	SAT

GOAL GETTER

☐ _____ ☐ _____ ☐ _____

THE WAY TO GET STARTED
IS TO QUIT TALKING
AND BEGIN DOING.
Walt Disney

IMPORTANT DATES

MONTHYLY RECAP

I'M PROUDEST OF MYSELF FOR

_____

_____

_____

I'M SO BRAVE FOR

_____

_____

_____

THE HARDEST THING I DID

_____

_____

_____

MY FAVORITE MEMORY

_____

_____

_____

YOU WILL FACE MANY DEFEATS IN YOUR LIFE,
BUT NEVER LET YURELF BE DEFEATED.

MAYA ANGELOU

I'VE GOT BIG PLANS

_____

_____

IMPORTANT
DATES NEXT
MONTH

A DREAM WRITTEN DOWN
BECOMES A GOAL.
A GOAL BROKEN DOWN
BECOMES A PLAN.
A PLAN BACKED BY
ACTION BECOMES
REALITY.

TRUST ME I HAVE A PLAN

Section 4.3
Weekly Planner

HOW TO SET UP THE WEEKLY PLANNER

Part of the Weekly Tracker is the Life Wheel! You Should Be Pretty Comfortable doing by now, so I'm not going to go over how to do them again. The Biggest Part of this Section is to Start Breaking Your Monthly Goal into a Weekly Goal. Again if You're not sure where to start looking at the First step of Step one in Your Where I am Activity in Section 3.4

WEEKLY OVERVIEW
WEEKLY GOALS

☐ CREATE A WEEKLY GOAL FROM
_____
WHERE I AM ACTIVITY
_____
☐ Pick a wake up time
_____

_____
☐
_____

GROW YOUR MIND
BOOK OR PODCAST

1 Mind Love Podcast   2 You Are a Badass (Jen Sincero)

BUILDING BETTER HABITS _____

Fill this out throughout the week or at the end!

S	M	T	W	T	F	S

THIS WEEK'S GREATEST ACCOMPLISHMENTS

_____
Fill this out at the end! _____
_____

I'M PROUD I TRIED

_____
_____
_____

NEXT WEEK I WILL

_____
_____

WEEKLY OVERVIEW
WEEKLY GOALS

☐ CREATE A WEEKLY GOAL FROM _____
   WHERE I AM ACTIVITY _____

☐ _____

_____

☐ _____

_____

GROW YOUR MIND
BOOK OR PODCAST

1 _____ 2 _____

BUILDING BETTER HABITS _____

S	M	T	W	T	F	S

THIS WEEK'S GREATEST ACCOMPLISHMENTS

_____

_____

_____

I'M PROUD I TRIED

_____

_____

_____

NEXT WEEK I WILL

_____

_____

LIFE WHEEL

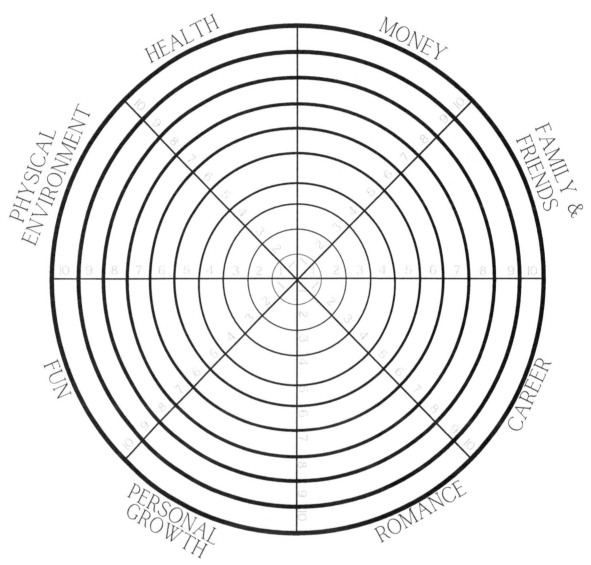

1: Worse than the Worst

2: The Worst

3: It doesn't look hopeful

4: It doesn't look good

5: It looks hopeful

6: Things are okay

7: Things are going pretty good

8: Things are going good

9: It's better than I thought

10: Life is a dream

I'M PROUD I SCORED HIGHEST IN: _____

_____

_____

NOW I'M GOING TO... _____

_____

_____

TO IMPROVE... _____

WEEKLY OVERVIEW
WEEKLY GOALS

☐ CREATE A WEEKLY GOAL FROM _____
   WHERE I AM ACTIVITY _____

☐ _____

_____

☐ _____

_____

GROW YOUR MIND
BOOK OR PODCAST

1 _____ 2 _____

BUILDING BETTER HABITS _____

S	M	T	W	T	F	S

THIS WEEK'S GREATEST ACCOMPLISHMENTS

_____

_____

_____

I'M PROUD I TRIED

_____

_____

_____

NEXT WEEK I WILL

_____

_____

LIFE WHEEL

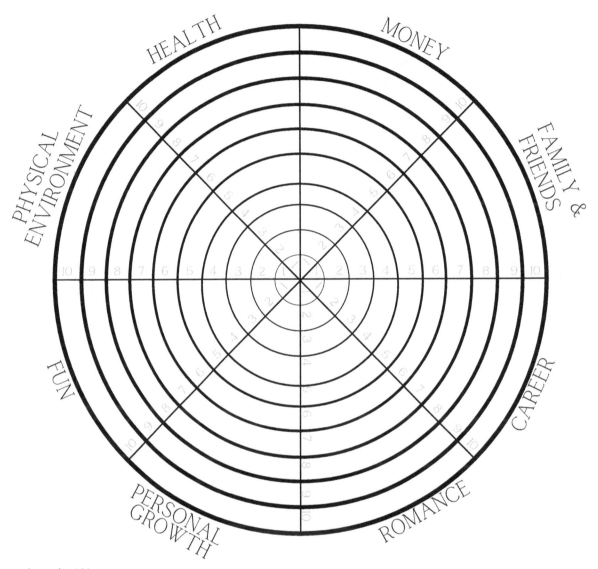

1: Worse than the Worst
2: The Worst
3: It doesn't look hopeful
4: It doesn't look good
5: It looks hopeful
6: Things are okay
7: Things are going pretty good
8: Things are going good
9: It's better than I thought
10: Life is a dream

I'M PROUD I SCORED HIGHEST IN: _____
_____
_____

NOW I'M GOING TO... _____
_____
_____

TO IMPROVE... _____

WEEKLY OVERVIEW
WEEKLY GOALS

☐ CREATE A WEEKLY GOAL FROM
_____
  WHERE I AM ACTIVITY
_____
☐ _____

_____
☐ _____

_____

GROW YOUR MIND
BOOK OR PODCAST

1 _____ 2 _____

BUILDING BETTER HABITS _____

S	M	T	W	T	F	S

THIS WEEK'S GREATEST ACCOMPLISHMENTS
_____
_____
_____

I'M PROUD I TRIED
_____
_____
_____

NEXT WEEK I WILL
_____
_____

LIFE WHEEL

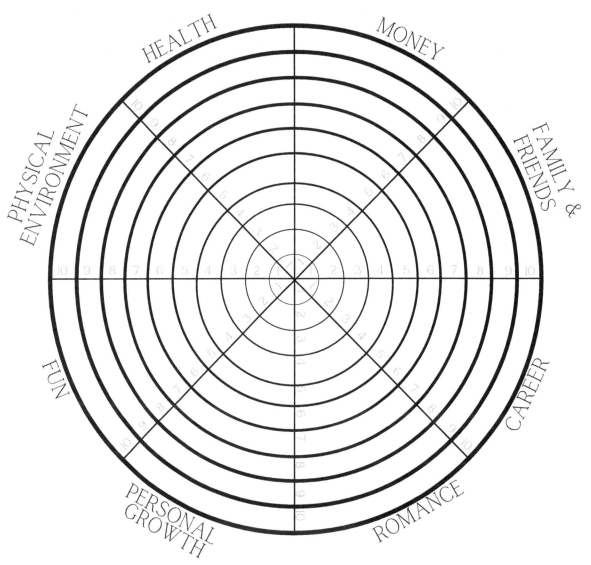

1: Worse than the Worst

2: The Worst

3: It doesn't look hopeful

4: It doesn't look good

5: It looks hopeful

6: Things are okay

7: Things are going pretty good

8: Things are going good

9: It's better than I thought

10: Life is a dream

I'M PROUD I SCORED HIGHEST IN: _____
_____
_____

NOW I'M GOING TO... _____
_____
_____

TO IMPROVE... _____

WEEKLY OVERVIEW
WEEKLY GOALS

☐ CREATE A WEEKLY GOAL FROM
  WHERE I AM ACTIVITY

☐ _____

_____

☐ _____

_____

GROW YOUR MIND
BOOK OR PODCAST

1 _____   2 _____

BUILDING BETTER HABITS _____

S	M	T	W	T	F	S

THIS WEEK'S GREATEST ACCOMPLISHMENTS

_____

_____

_____

I'M PROUD I TRIED

_____

_____

NEXT WEEK I WILL

_____

_____

LIFE WHEEL

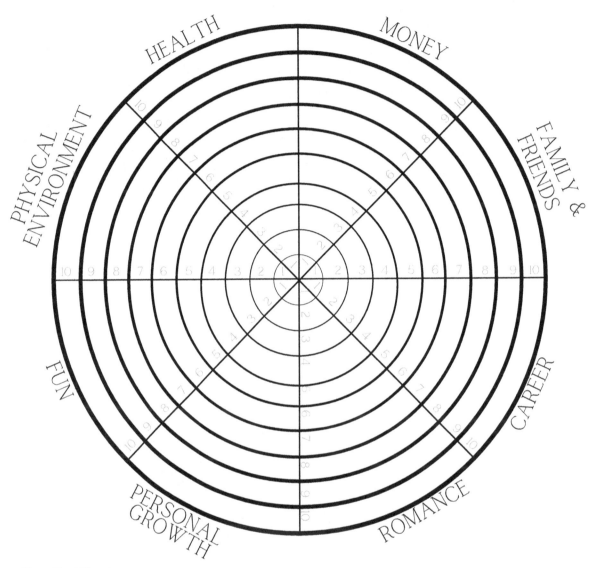

1: Worse than the Worst

2: The Worst

3: It doesn't look hopeful

4: It doesn't look good

5: It looks hopeful

6: Things are okay

7: Things are going pretty good

8: Things are going good

9: It's better than I thought

10: Life is a dream

I'M PROUD I SCORED HIGHEST IN:

_____

_____

_____

NOW I'M GOING TO...

_____

_____

TO IMPROVE...

I AM WORTH
OF LIVING A LIFE
THAT FEELS LIKE A
DREAM I DON'T
WANT TO
WAKE UP FROM

TAKE IT A DAY AT A TIME

Section 4.3

Daily Planner

HOW TO SET UP THE DAILY PLANNER

Much like the monthly and the Weekly Planner the Biggest Part of this Planner is creating a Daily Goal! I also want to note that this Planner is designed for you to skip days and pick up where you left off. So if you miss a day, don't be afraid to come back to it when you are fresh and ready to give it another go! Remember consistency is more about being committed than doing it every day!

It is also designed to be filled out throughout the day which I go over in the example on the next page!

MONTH   DAY   YEAR

6:00	
6:30	
7:00	
7:30	
8:00	
8:30	
9:00	** Fill out
9:30	After You
10:00	Do Your
10:30	Top 3
11:00	Goals
11:30	
12:00	
12:30	
1:00	
1:30	
2:00	
2:30	
3:00	
3:30	
4:00	
4:30	
5:00	
5:30	
6:00	
6:30	
7:00	
7:30	
8:00	
8:30	
9:00	
9:30	
10:00	
10:30	

TOP 3 GOALS

☐ WHAT IS MY BIGGEST GOAL?

☐ Select a wake up time

*Fill out in the first thing in the Morning or Night Before

MORNING ROUTINE

☐ WAKE UP
☐ DRINK WATER
☐ MOVE BODY (YOGA - WALK)

PICK 1 MID DAY BREAK

☐ HEALTHY SNACK - MEDITATE - WALK -
CALL A FRIEND - FUN PODCAST/BOOK

TODAY I WILL

☐ Whatever else I need to Do!
☐
☐
☐
☐

DRINK UP

16 OZ   16 OZ

16 OZ   16 OZ

16 OZ   16 OZ

BRAIN DUMP

For those who don't like to write...

ONE THING FOR MY GOAL

*** Everything from this Line Down Gets filled out at night!

ONE HARD THING I DID

WHAT I DID FOR ME

I AM GRATEFUL FOR

TODAY'S WINS

EVENING ROUTINE

☐ BRUSH TEETH
☐ TODAYS WINS
☐ GRATITUDE

MONTH   DAY   YEAR
_____

TOP 3 GOALS

☐ WHAT IS MY BIGGEST
   GOAL?
   _____

☐ _____

   _____

☐ _____

MORNING ROUTINE

☐ WAKE UP
☐ DRINK WATER
☐ MOVE BODY (YOGA - WALK)

PICK 1 MID DAY BREAK

☐ HEALTHY SNACK - MEDITATE - WALK -
  CALL A FRIEND - FUN PODCAST/BOOK

TODAY I WILL

☐ _____
☐ _____
☐ _____
☐ _____
☐ _____

DRINK UP

16 OZ   16 OZ

16 OZ   16 OZ

16 OZ   16 OZ

BRAIN DUMP

ONE THING
FOR MY GOAL _____

ONE HARD   WHAT I DID
THING I DID   FOR ME
_____

I AM GRATEFUL FOR
_____
_____
_____
_____
_____

TODAY'S WINS
_____
_____
_____
_____

EVENING ROUTINE

☐ BRUSH TEETH
☐ TODAY'S WINS
☐ GRATITUDE

6:00	
6:30	
7:00	
7:30	
8:00	
8:30	
9:00	
9:30	
10:00	
10:30	
11:00	
11:30	
12:00	
12:30	
1:00	
1:30	
2:00	
2:30	
3:00	
3:30	
4:00	
4:30	
5:00	
5:30	
6:00	
6:30	
7:00	
7:30	
8:00	
8:30	
9:00	
9:30	
10:00	
10:30	

DAILY AFFIRMATIONS

I AM

_____
_____
_____
_____
_____

I HAVE

_____
_____
_____
_____
_____

MY WHY

_____
_____
_____

I AM GRATEFUL FOR

_____
_____
_____
_____
_____
_____
_____

I AM SO HAPPY & GRATEFUL NOW THAT

_____
_____
_____
_____

MONTH   DAY   YEAR

6:00	
6:30	
7:00	
7:30	
8:00	
8:30	
9:00	
9:30	
10:00	
10:30	
11:00	
11:30	
12:00	
12:30	
1:00	
1:30	
2:00	
2:30	
3:00	
3:30	
4:00	
4:30	
5:00	
5:30	
6:00	
6:30	
7:00	
7:30	
8:00	
8:30	
9:00	
9:30	
10:00	
10:30	

TOP 3 GOALS

☐ WHAT IS MY FRIST
   STEP FOR THAT GOAL?

☐ _____

☐ _____

MORNING ROUTINE

☐ WAKE UP
☐ DRINK WATER
☐ MOVE BODY (YOGA - WALK)

PICK 1 MID DAY BREAK

☐ HEALTHY SNACK - MEDITATE - WALK -
   CALL A FRIEND - FUN PODCAST/BOOK

TODAY I WILL

☐ _____
☐ _____
☐ _____
☐ _____
☐ _____

DRINK UP

16 OZ   16 OZ
16 OZ   16 OZ
16 OZ   16 OZ

BRAIN DUMP

ONE THING
FOR MY GOAL

ONE HARD
THING I DID

WHAT I DID
FOR ME

I AM GRATEFUL FOR

TODAY'S WINS

EVENING ROUTINE

☐ BRUSH TEETH
☐ TODAY'S WINS
☐ GRATITUDE

DAILY AFFIRMATIONS

I AM

_____
_____
_____
_____

I HAVE

_____
_____
_____
_____

MY WHY

_____
_____
_____

I AM GRATEFUL FOR

_____
_____
_____
_____
_____
_____

I AM SO HAPPY & GRATEFUL NOW THAT

_____
_____
_____
_____

MONTH _____ DAY _____ YEAR _____

| 6:00 _____ |
| 6:30 _____ |
| 7:00 _____ |
| 7:30 _____ |
| 8:00 _____ |
| 8:30 _____ |

TOP 3 GOALS

☐ WHAT DO I NEED TO
　 START MY FIRST STEP _____

☐ _____

_____

☐ _____

MORNING ROUTINE

☐ WAKE UP _____
☐ DRINK WATER _____
☐ MOVE BODY (YOGA - WALK) _____

PICK 1 MID DAY BREAK

☐ HEALTHY SNACK - MEDITATE - WALK -
　 CALL A FRIEND - FUN PODCAST/BOOK

| 9:00 _____ |
| 9:30 _____ |
| 10:00 _____ |
| 10:30 _____ |
| 11:00 _____ |
| 11:30 _____ |
| 12:00 _____ |
| 12:30 _____ |

TODAY I WILL

☐ _____
☐ _____
☐ _____
☐ _____
☐ _____

DRINK UP

[16 OZ] [16 OZ]

[16 OZ] [16 OZ]

[16 OZ] [16 OZ]

| 1:00 _____ |
| 1:30 _____ |
| 2:00 _____ |
| 2:30 _____ |
| 3:00 _____ |
| 3:30 _____ |
| 4:00 _____ |
| 4:30 _____ |
| 5:00 _____ |
| 5:30 _____ |

BRAIN DUMP

┌─────────────────────────┐
│   │
│   │
│   │
│   │
│   │
└─────────────────────────┘

| 6:00 _____ |
| 6:30 _____ |
| 7:00 _____ |
| 7:30 _____ |
| 8:00 _____ |
| 8:30 _____ |
| 9:00 _____ |
| 9:30 _____ |
| 10:00 _____ |
| 10:30 _____ |

ONE THING
FOR MY GOAL _____

ONE HARD
THING I DID

_____

_____

WHAT I DID
FOR ME

I AM GRATEFUL FOR

_____

_____

_____

_____

TODAY'S WINS

_____

_____

_____

_____

EVENING ROUTINE

☐ BRUSH TEETH _____
☐ TODAY'S WINS _____
☐ GRATITUDE _____

DAILY AFFIRMATIONS

I AM

_____
_____
_____
_____

I HAVE

_____
_____
_____
_____

MY WHY

_____
_____
_____

I AM GRATEFUL FOR

_____
_____
_____
_____
_____
_____

I AM SO HAPPY & GRATEFUL NOW THAT

_____
_____
_____

MONTH _____ DAY ___ YEAR ___

TOP 3 GOALS

☐ PLAN A TO DO MY FRIST STEP
_____

☐ _____

_____

☐ _____

MORNING ROUTINE

☐ WAKE UP _____
☐ DRINK WATER _____
☐ MOVE BODY (YOGA - WALK)

PICK 1 MID DAY BREAK

☐ HEALTHY SNACK - MEDITATE - WALK -
CALL A FRIEND - FUN PODCAST/BOOK

TODAY I WILL

☐ _____
☐ _____
☐ _____
☐ _____
☐ _____

DRINK UP

16 OZ   16 OZ

16 OZ   16 OZ

16 OZ   16 OZ

BRAIN DUMP

_____

ONE THING FOR MY GOAL _____

ONE HARD THING I DID
_____
_____

WHAT I DID FOR ME _____

I AM GRATEFUL FOR
_____
_____
_____
_____
_____

TODAY'S WINS
_____
_____
_____
_____

EVENING ROUTINE

☐ BRUSH TEETH
☐ TODAY'S WINS
☐ GRATITUDE

6:00	
6:30	
7:00	
7:30	
8:00	
8:30	
9:00	
9:30	
10:00	
10:30	
11:00	
11:30	
12:00	
12:30	
1:00	
1:30	
2:00	
2:30	
3:00	
3:30	
4:00	
4:30	
5:00	
5:30	
6:00	
6:30	
7:00	
7:30	
8:00	
8:30	
9:00	
9:30	
10:00	
10:30	

DAILY AFFIRMATIONS

I AM

_____

_____

_____

_____

I HAVE

_____

_____

_____

_____

MY WHY

_____

_____

_____

I AM GRATEFUL FOR

_____

_____

_____

_____

_____

_____

I AM SO HAPPY & GRATEFUL NOW THAT

_____

_____

_____

MONTH   DAY   YEAR

TOP 3 GOALS

☐ PLAN B TO DO MY FRIST STEP

☐ _____

☐ _____

MORNING ROUTINE

☐ WAKE UP
☐ DRINK WATER
☐ MOVE BODY (YOGA - WALK)

PICK 1 MID DAY BREAK

☐ HEALTHY SNACK - MEDITATE - WALK -
CALL A FRIEND - FUN PODCAST/BOOK

TODAY I WILL

☐ _____
☐ _____
☐ _____
☐ _____
☐ _____

DRINK UP

16 OZ   16 OZ

16 OZ   16 OZ

16 OZ   16 OZ

BRAIN DUMP

ONE THING
FOR MY GOAL _____

ONE HARD
THING I DID

_____

EVENING ROUTINE

☐ BRUSH TEETH
☐ TODAY'S WINS
☐ GRATITUDE

WHAT I DID
FOR ME

I AM GRATEFUL FOR

_____
_____
_____
_____
_____

TODAY'S WINS

_____
_____
_____
_____

6:00
6:30
7:00
7:30
8:00
8:30
9:00
9:30
10:00
10:30
11:00
11:30
12:00
12:30
1:00
1:30
2:00
2:30
3:00
3:30
4:00
4:30
5:00
5:30
6:00
6:30
7:00
7:30
8:00
8:30
9:00
9:30
10:00
10:30

DAILY AFFIRMATIONS

I AM

_____
_____
_____
_____

I HAVE

_____
_____
_____
_____

MY WHY

_____
_____
_____

I AM GRATEFUL FOR

_____
_____
_____
_____
_____

I AM SO HAPPY & GRATEFUL NOW THAT

_____
_____
_____

MONTH _____ DAY _____ YEAR _____

TOP 3 GOALS

☐ MY OH SHI*T PLAN TO
DO MY FIRST STEP

☐ _____

_____

☐ _____

MORNING ROUTINE

☐ WAKE UP

☐ DRINK WATER

☐ MOVE BODY (YOGA - WALK)

PICK 1 MID DAY BREAK

☐ HEALTHY SNACK - MEDITATE - WALK -
CALL A FRIEND - FUN PODCAST/BOOK

TODAY I WILL

☐ _____
☐ _____
☐ _____
☐ _____
☐ _____

DRINK UP

16 OZ   16 OZ

16 OZ   16 OZ

16 OZ   16 OZ

BRAIN DUMP

[ ]

ONE THING FOR MY GOAL
_____

ONE HARD THING I DID
_____
_____

WHAT I DID FOR ME
_____

I AM GRATEFUL FOR
_____
_____
_____
_____
_____

TODAY'S WINS
_____
_____
_____
_____

EVENING ROUTINE

☐ BRUSH TEETH

☐ TODAY'S WINS

☐ GRATITUDE

6:00 _____
6:30 _____
7:00 _____
7:30 _____
8:00 _____
8:30 _____
9:00 _____
9:30 _____
10:00 _____
10:30 _____
11:00 _____
11:30 _____
12:00 _____
12:30 _____
1:00 _____
1:30 _____
2:00 _____
2:30 _____
3:00 _____
3:30 _____
4:00 _____
4:30 _____
5:00 _____
5:30 _____
6:00 _____
6:30 _____
7:00 _____
7:30 _____
8:00 _____
8:30 _____
9:00 _____
9:30 _____
10:00 _____
10:30 _____

DAILY AFFIRMATIONS

I AM

_____

_____

_____

_____

I HAVE

_____

_____

_____

_____

MY WHY

_____

_____

_____

I AM GRATEFUL FOR

_____

_____

_____

_____

_____

_____

I AM SO HAPPY & GRATEFUL NOW THAT

_____

_____

_____

_____

MONTH   DAY   YEAR

6:00
6:30
7:00
7:30

TOP 3 GOALS

☐ CELEBRATE ME
   TODAY

☐ _____

☐ _____

MORNING ROUTINE

☐ WAKE UP
☐ DRINK WATER
☐ MOVE BODY (YOGA - WALK)

PICK 1 MID DAY BREAK

☐ HEALTHY SNACK - MEDITATE - WALK -
  CALL A FRIEND - FUN PODCAST/BOOK

8:00
8:30
9:00
9:30
10:00
10:30
11:00
11:30
12:00
12:30

TODAY I WILL

☐ _____
☐ _____
☐ _____
☐ _____
☐ _____

DRINK UP

16 OZ   16 OZ

16 OZ   16 OZ

16 OZ   16 OZ

1:00
1:30
2:00
2:30
3:00
3:30
4:00
4:30
5:00
5:30

BRAIN DUMP

6:00
6:30
7:00
7:30
8:00
8:30
9:00

ONE THING
FOR MY GOAL

9:30
10:00
10:30

ONE HARD
THING I DID

WHAT I DID
FOR ME

_____

I AM GRATEFUL FOR

TODAY'S WINS

EVENING ROUTINE

☐ BRUSH TEETH
☐ TODAY'S WINS
☐ GRATITUDE

DAILY AFFIRMATIONS

I AM

_____
_____
_____
_____

I HAVE

_____
_____
_____
_____

MY WHY

_____
_____
_____

I AM GRATEFUL FOR

_____
_____
_____
_____
_____
_____

I AM SO HAPPY & GRATEFUL NOW THAT

_____
_____
_____

SOMEDAY YOU WILL
MEET THE HAPPIEST
VERSION OF
YOURSELF.
AND IT WILL BE
WORTH IT

LET'S GET TRACKING

Section 4.4

Monthly Trackers

HOW TO SET UP THE MONTHLY TRACKERS

I put these Monthly Trackers in as a Bonus for us! They're pretty self-explanatory and the examples will help guide you through if you have any questions. But I did want to mention, while these are monthly trackers they're designed to be used weekly. Preferably once a week when possible! They give you a new overview of the whole month which can be super helpful!

SPENDING
TRACKER

INCOME

SOURCE	AMOUNT
Job	$4000
Esty	$500

WISHLIST

New Phone
Road Trip

I WILL SAVE: $500

DATE	DESCRIPTIONS	AMOUNT
10/1	Pumpkin Spice Latte	$5.58
10/5	Target Run	$67.43

SPENDING
TRACKER

INCOME

SOURCE	AMOUNT

WISHLIST

I WILL SAVE: _____

DATE	DESCRIPTIONS	AMOUNT

HABIT TRACKER

MY NEW HABIT: Yoga in the Morning

WHY THIS NEW HABIT IS IMPORTANT
I want to feel healthier and start my day off with
something for me!

✎	M	✎	✎	T	F	✎

REWARD A new Yoga Mat!

S	✎	T	✎	✎	F	S

REWARD Take myself out for Coffee

S	M	T	W	T	F	S

REWARD

S	M	T	W	T	F	S

REWARD

HABIT TRACKER

MY NEW HABIT:_____

WHY THIS NEW HABIT IS IMPORTANT
_____
_____
_____

S	M	T	W	T	F	S

REWARD _____

S	M	T	W	T	F	S

REWARD _____

S	M	T	W	T	F	S

REWARD _____

S	M	T	W	T	F	S

REWARD _____

FITNESS TRACKER

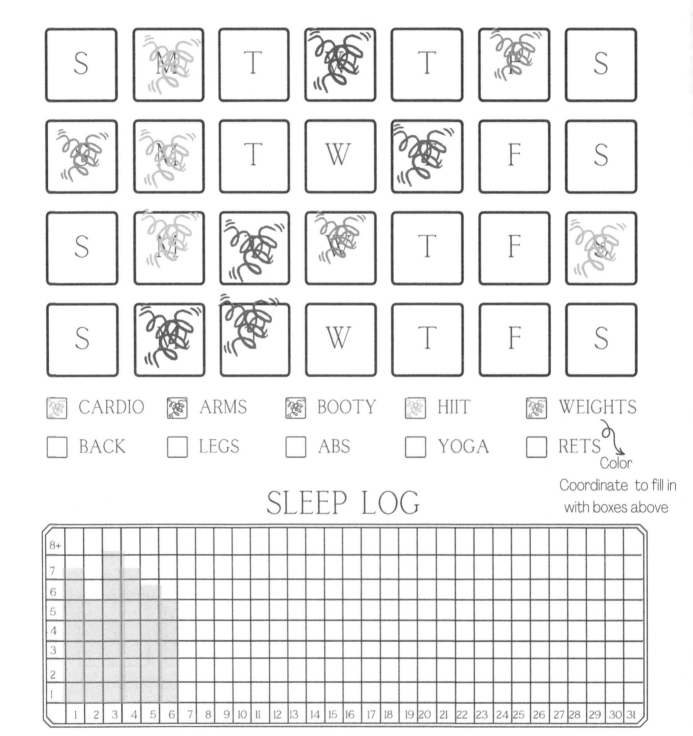

S	M	T		T		S
	M	T	W		F	S
S	M			T	F	
S			W	T	F	S

- ▨ CARDIO
- ▨ ARMS
- ▨ BOOTY
- ▨ HIIT
- ▨ WEIGHTS
- ☐ BACK
- ☐ LEGS
- ☐ ABS
- ☐ YOGA
- ☐ RETS

Color
Coordinate to fill in
with boxes above

SLEEP LOG

	1	2	3	4	5	6	7	8	9	10	11	12	13	14	15	16	17	18	19	20	21	22	23	24	25	26	27	28	29	30	31
8+																															
7																															
6																															
5																															
4																															
3																															
2																															
1																															

FITNESS TRACKER

S	M	T	W	T	F	S
S	M	T	W	T	F	S
S	M	T	W	T	F	S
S	M	T	W	T	F	S

☐ CARDIO ☐ ARMS ☐ BOOTY ☐ HIIT ☐ WEIGHTS

☐ BACK ☐ LEGS ☐ ABS ☐ YOGA ☐ RETS

SLEEP LOG

	1	2	3	4	5	6	7	8	9	10	11	12	13	14	15	16	17	18	19	20	21	22	23	24	25	26	27	28	29	30	31
8+																																
7																																
6																																
5																																
4																																
3																																
2																																
1																																

CLEANING TRACKER

DAILY

Make Bed

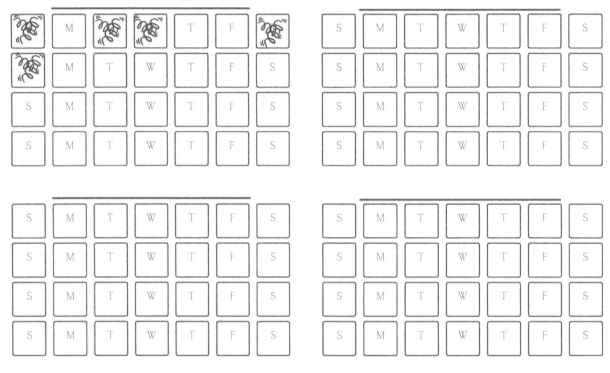

WEEKLY

Laundry

| | WK 2 | WK 3 | WK 4 | | WK 1 | WK 2 | WK 3 | WK 4 | | WK 1 | WK 2 | WK 3 | WK 4 |

MONTHLY

☐ Kitchen ☐ _____ ☐ _____

☐ _____ ☐ _____ ☐ _____

CLEANING TRACKER

DAILY

S	M	T	W	T	F	S
S	M	T	W	T	F	S
S	M	T	W	T	F	S
S	M	T	W	T	F	S

S	M	T	W	T	F	S
S	M	T	W	T	F	S
S	M	T	W	T	F	S
S	M	T	W	T	F	S

S	M	T	W	T	F	S
S	M	T	W	T	F	S
S	M	T	W	T	F	S
S	M	T	W	T	F	S

S	M	T	W	T	F	S
S	M	T	W	T	F	S
S	M	T	W	T	F	S
S	M	T	W	T	F	S

WEEKLY

WK 1	WK 2	WK 3	WK 4

WK 1	WK 2	WK 3	WK 4

WK 1	WK 2	WK 3	WK 4

MONTHLY

TIME TO CLOSE IT DOWN

Section 4.4

Finale & Reference Pages

YOU DID IT!

& Now You Keep Doing it...

First, I want you to go SO hard - go big and celebrate all you've accomplished! I know how life-changing these activities can be, but changing your life is no easy task. Tou did it! (and you're still doing it!)

Just because this workbook has ended I don't want you to stop using what you learned or the planner! I know you've done so much work already, but the truth is the work has really just started! It's going to be a crazy road ahead but the journey will most certainly be worth it!

Keep at it and don't lose sight of Your 'Why'.

I know you are meant to do amazing things and leave your impact in your own unique way!

And when it gets hard ask yourself, would I regret giving up now?

I am so excited for you to take this new step and to see where life takes you!

REFERENCE

<u>Personality Tests Websites</u>

"*"It's so Incredible to Finally Be Understood.".*" *16Personalities*, NERIS Analytics Limited, 2011, www.16personalities.com/.

"*The Enneagram Personality Test.*" *Truity*, Truity, 2020, www.truity.com/test/enneagram-personality-test.

<u>Fear Setting</u>

Ferris, Tim. "*Chapter 3 - Dodging Bullets: Fear Setting and Escaping Paralysis.*" *The 4-Hour Workweek*, Crown Publishing Group, 2007.

<u>Deam Mapping (Dreamlining)</u>

Ferris, Tim. "*Chapter 4 - System Rest: Being Unreasonable and Unambiguous.*" *The 4-Hour Workweek*, Crown Publishing Group), 2007.

<u>Action Board</u>

<u>Swart, Tara. "*Chapter 13: Step 2: Action Board It.*" The Source, HarperCollins Publishers, 2019.-</u>

CLOSING WORDS...

I want to say thank you to everyone who supported me to get to this
point. For those who stuck with me even when I was still going for my
dreams like a crazy person with nothing to my name, THANK YOU!
I also want to give a shout-out to my coaches and therapist who guided
and encouraged me every day.
Lastly, I want to thank you. If there wasn't someone crazy enough to
believe in themselves and their dream I would never be able to live mine!
Thank you for believing in yourself and for being one of the bold ones who
will look back and be proud of the life they lived!

Made in the USA
Las Vegas, NV
14 June 2022

50224639R10109